BODY IMAGE AND IDENTITY IN CONTEMPORARY SOCIETIES

Popular interest in body image issues has grown dramatically in recent years, due to an emphasis on individual responsibility and self-determination in contemporary society as well as the seemingly limitless capacities of modern medicine; however, body image as a separate field of academic inquiry is still relatively young. The contributors of *Body Image and Identity in Contemporary Societies* explore the complex social, political and aesthetic interconnections between body image and identity. It is an in-depth study that allows for new perspectives in the analysis of contemporary visual art and literature but also reflects on how these social constructs inform clinical treatment.

Sukhanova and Thomashoff bring together contributions from psychoanalysts, psychotherapists, psychiatrists and scholars in the fields of the social sciences and the humanities to explore representations of the body in literature and the arts across different times and cultures. The chapters analyse the social construction of the 'ideal' body in terms of beauty, gender, sexuality, race, ethnicity, class and disability, from a broadly psychoanalytic perspective, and trace the mechanisms which define the role of physical appearance in the formation of identity and the assumption of social roles.

The unique interdisciplinary outlook of *Body Image and Identity in Contemporary Societies* aims to bridge the current gap between clinical observations and research in semiotic theory. It will be of interest to psychoanalysts, psychotherapists, art therapists, art theorists, academics in the humanities and social sciences, and those interested in an interdisciplinary approach to the issues of body image and identity.

Ekaterina Sukhanova is University Director of Academic Program Review at the City University of New York, USA. She serves as Scientific Secretary of the Section for Art and Psychiatry and the Section of Art and Psychiatry of the World Psychiatric Association. She is also engaged in interdisciplinary research on cultural constructs of mental health and illness and curates exhibitions of art brut as a vehicle for fighting stigma.

Hans-Otto Thomashoff was born in Germany and lives in Vienna. He is a psychiatrist, psychoanalyst, art historian and author of fiction and non-fiction books. He has been curator of several art exhibitions highlighting the connection between the psyche and art as well as President of the Section of Art and Psychiatry of the World Psychiatric Association and advisory committee member of the Sigmund Freud Foundation, Vienna.

BODY IMAGE AND IDENTITY IN CONTEMPORARY SOCIETIES

Psychoanalytic, social, cultural and aesthetic perspectives

Edited by Ekaterina Sukhanova and Hans-Otto Thomashoff

Routledge
Taylor & Francis Group
LONDON AND NEW YORK

First published 2015
by Routledge
27 Church Road, Hove, East Sussex, BN3 2FA

and by Routledge
711 Third Avenue, New York, NY 10017

Routledge is an imprint of the Taylor & Francis Group, an informa business

British Library Cataloguing in Publication Data
A catalogue record for this book is available from the British Library

Library of Congress Cataloging in Publication Data
Body image and identity in contemporary societies : psychoanalytic, social, cultural and aesthetic perspectives / edited by Hans-Otto Thomashoff and Ekaterina Sukhanova.
pages cm
Includes bibliographical references and index.
1. Body image. 2. Identity (Psychology) I. Thomashoff, Hans-Otto, editor. II. Sukhanova, Ekaterina, editor.
BF697.5.B63B61853 2015
306.4′613--dc23
2014034878

ISBN: 978-0-415-74290-0 (hbk)
ISBN: 978-0-415-74291-7 (pbk)
ISBN: 978-1-315-72418-8 (ebk)

Typeset in Bembo
by Saxon Graphics Ltd, Derby

CONTENTS

CONTRIBUTORS

Anne Brun, Ph.D.
Professor of Psychopathology and Clinical Psychology

Director of the Centre for Research in Psychopathology and Clinical Psychology, University Lumière-Lyon 2, Lyons, France

Angélique Christaki, Ph.D.
Psychoanalyst and Clinical Psychologist

Associated Researcher and Lecturer, University of Paris VII Diderot, Paris, France

Catherine Desprats Péquignot, Ph.D.
Practicing Clinical Psychologist and Psychoanalyst

Associate Professor of Clinical Psychopathology and Psychoanalysis, University of Paris VII Diderot, Paris, France

William Ebenstein, Ph.D.
University Dean for Health and Human Services, City University of New York, New York, USA

Alcira Forero-Peña, Ph.D.
Adjunct Assistant Professor in Anthropology, City University of New York, New York, USA

Alexander Kopytin, Ph.D.
Associate Professor,
Academy of Post-Graduate Pedagogical Education and North-West Medical Mechnikov University, St. Petersburg, Russia

Vice-Chair of the Section on Art and Psychiatry,
World Psychiatric Association

Simone Korff Sausse, Ph.D.
Practicing Clinical Psychologist and Psychoanalyst
Associate Professor, Psychoanalytical Studies,
University of Paris VII Diderot, Paris, France

Céline Masson, Ph.D.
Practicing Psychoanalyst, Associate Professor of Clinical Psychopathology and Psychoanalysis,
University of Paris VII Diderot, Paris, France

Clinical Psychologist,
Socio-Medical Center OSE, Paris, France

Renata Mattos-Avril, Ph.D.
Doctor in Psychoanalysis,
Rio de Janeiro State University, Rio de Janeiro, Brazil

Post-Doctoral Researcher,
University of Nice Sophia-Antipolis, Nice, France

Rémy Potier, Ph.D.
Clinical Psychologist, Practicing Psychoanalyst and Associate Professor, Psychopathology,
University of Paris VII Diderot, Paris, France

Silke Schauder, Ph.D.
Professor of Clinical Psychology and Psychopathology,
University de Picardie Jules Verne, Amiens, France

Ekaterina Sukhanova, Ph.D.
University Director, Academic Program Review, Articulation and Transfer,
City University of New York, New York, USA

Vice-President, Section on Art and Psychiatry
Secretary, Section on Literature and Psychiatry
World Psychiatric Association

Hans-Otto Thomashoff, M.D., Ph.D.
Psychiatrist, Psychoanalyst, Art Historian;
Advisory Committee Member, Sigmund Freud Foundation, Vienna, Austria

President of the Section on Art and Psychiatry,
World Psychiatric Association

Jean-Michel Vives, Ph.D.
Professor of Clinical and Pathological Psychology,
University of Nice Sophia-Antipolis, Nice, France

Régine Waintrater, Ph.D.
Psychoanalyst, Associate Professor,
University of Paris VII Diderot, Paris, France

Jeanne Wolff Bernstein, Ph.D.
Practicing Psychoanalyst, Faculty Member,
The Psychoanalytic Institute of Northern California, USA

Practicing Psychoanalyst, Faculty Member,
Sigmund Freud University, Vienna, Austria

FROM THE EDITORS

> How could one express in words these emotions of the body?
>
> Virginia Woolf

The common theme of this collective volume is the exploration of the complex social, cultural and aesthetic interconnections between body image and identity. The mechanisms defining the role of physical appearance in the developing of an identity and the assumption of social roles involve many contexts: the ideal of beauty, gender roles, ethnic stereotypes, cultural perception of mental and physical disabilities, and so forth. An in-depth study of these mechanisms not only allows for new perspectives in the analysis of contemporary visual art and literature but also invites us to reflect on how these social constructs inform the clinical enterprise.

The contributors represent different academic specialties: psychotherapists, psychiatrists and scholars in the fields of humanities and social sciences. Through multidisciplinary and intercultural lenses, this volume addresses several overarching themes in the interconnections between body image and selfhood. How does body image affect the construction of contemporary identity? What human experiences, behaviours and clinical practices influence this process of identity formation? What role do the social constructs of the norm, pathology and disability play in the understanding of identity in modern society? How does the 'imaginary' metaphorical body as the subject of art correlate with the actual physical body as the subject of medicine or science?

The volume opens with a selection of articles establishing a broad theoretical and historical context of the body as a psychosocial phenomenon. The chapter by Hans-Otto Thomashoff addresses the overarching issues of biological and psychological bases of creativity. His examination of the relationship between creativity and cognitive and emotional development offers a link to the clinical approach to psychopathologies of body experiences.

Ekaterina Sukhanova's chapter introduces a semiotic theory approach to explore the notion of aesthetic norm as applied to the field of outsider art. Sukhanova establishes the connection between the semiotic mechanisms of art production and perception that underpin the potential of art to counteract stigma, including self-stigmatisation. Angélique Christaki offers an insightful theoretical overview of body image in psychoanalysis and its link to the domain of art. Rémy Potier investigates the permeable borders between the art of medicine and contemporary art leading to new manifestations of the virtual body.

Several authors explore body image through the prism of trauma, related to objective deviations of body competence or experiences of physical aggression. William Ebenstein considers the impact of disability on the subjective experiences of body and self from a historical sociocultural perspective, while Simone Korff Sausse approaches the handicap concept, utilising a psychodynamic approach situated in gender studies. Régine Waintrater examines the respective functions of the bodily schema and body image in the context of relationships that victims of extreme violence and torture have to their self.

The next section focuses on the self-creation of appearance and body experience through specific works of visual arts, performing arts or literature: Michael Jackson (Silke Schauder), Carolee Schneemann (Catherine Desprats Péquignot), Gunther Von Hagens (Céline Masson), Hervé Guibert (Anne Brun). Renata Mattos-Avril and Jean-Michel Vives analyse the evolution of the classical notion of catharsis in contemporary theatre as a symptom of the shifting relations between body and identity in the postdramatic era.

The political and social dimensions of body image constructs is considered in the chapter by Alcira Forero-Peña, which captures the gender-linked issues of cosmetic surgery as a body image intervention. Jeanne Wolff Bernstein's chapter provides a thought-provoking examination of tattoos as a social tool and as a tangible sign of internal psychic conflicts. Alexander Kopytin's chapter capitalises on his clinical experience, investigating the use of humour as part of reconstructing body image in clinical art therapy. While the grotesque body alterations are purely symbolic rather than tangible as in the case of elective surgery and tattoos discussed in the preceding articles, such drawings may also be considered to be aimed at altering the self-concept through bodily changes.

Many articles transcend the boundaries of a single academic discipline, bearing witness to the multifaceted and dynamic nature of body image constructs. The book's aim is to promote the bridging of disciplinary gaps between clinical or biomedical observations and research in art theory, humanities, and social sciences.

Ekaterina Sukhanova and Hans-Otto Thomashoff

1

HOW THE BRAIN CREATES ART AND DREAMS

Hans-Otto Thomashoff

In the following chapter I would like to address some fundamental questions:

Why does the brain produce art? What are the influences of the brain on art production? How do biology and psychology jointly form art and dreams? How does art reflect the self perception of the artist?

The task of the brain is to produce an image of the outer reality that (usually) allows for a reasonable coping mechanism. Each living creature depends on keeping a balance of its bodily functions; without such balance, it dies. While in plants, direct cell-to-cell contact is enough to assure the distribution of water and nutrition, animals already at the level of the first multicellular organisms began to develop a nervous system as a coordination system for the tasks needed for survival. In the beginning this was very primitive. Its only task was to assure the supply of oxygen, water and food. As evolution progressed, its tasks expanded: sex for the preservation of the species, maintenance of a stable body temperature, breathing, and hormonal systems, just to mention a few. All these functions depend on a central regulation.

Human beings so far have the most elaborate nervous system. Headed by the brain, its activity has become so complex that we have gained a consciousness and define ourselves as humans largely as a result of the brain's activities. Consecutively the main criterion for the death of the person is the end of all brain activity.

Whilst most of the numerous brain functions never become conscious to us, some tasks demand purposeful actions and depend, at least to some extent, on conscious decision-making. Finding water, food or sexual partners requires active behaviour in the world we live in. By means of the hormonal systems the brain processes imbalances which result in sensations like hunger, thirst or sexual lust and strongly demand actions to reinstate the original balance. We have to actively drink to quench our thirst and maybe even do something to find water to start with. (Personally I love the strategy of the Kalahari bushman in the Jamie Uys film

Animals are Beautiful People: he catches a baboon, feeds it with salt and then lets it sit and wait all night bound to a tree. The next morning the poor animal is so thirsty, that when the bushman lets it free, it non-stop runs to its hidden source of fresh water leading its torturer to it.) Also finding food can depend on various more or less creative activities, even if you are not French, not to mention the satisfaction of our sexual desires.

At some point the increasing complexity of thinking resulted in an expansion of its tasks beyond simply securing basic physical needs. Fantasy, and with it a psychological reality, evolved. Even though inevitably linked to the body, the psychological system developed needs on its own. Without external stimuli, without mental nutrition, we cannot exist.

Imagine you are offered a job where the only thing you have to do is: nothing. In exchange you receive a generous salary. Would you say no? Sounds tempting, doesn't it? Canada, 1954: long lines of people were waiting outside to be able to participate in a psychological experiment which exactly demanded of them to do nothing. They just had to rest in bed with their hands and legs loosely tied and their eyes focused on the ceiling. Food and drink was served as desired, and at any point in time they could resign.

Most of the participants took the chance to sleep. When they woke up again, they started to sing or whistle after a while. Or they started talking to themselves. After a couple of hours they began to feel discomfort. Even though it meant waiving their salary, the first ones stepped out. Those who stayed up to 24 hours all began to hallucinate. The experiment had to be terminated prematurely. The participants who stayed until just before the end were not able to resign themselves, they all were acutely psychotic (Hacker 1971: 179). Deprived from external stimuli, our psychological balance is disturbed, just as our physical balance is without food or water.

Not only a severe deterioration of our physical stability leads to death, but also a massive disturbance of our psychological demands. As a result, suicide is the eighth most common cause of death in human beings, in the age group between 15 to 24 it is even rated second. In the United States alone, each year 30,000 people commit suicide – that is one every 18 minutes (Andreasen 2001: 553). But what evolutionary benefit do we get from a brain that makes us dependent on the environment and creates an enormous risk for survival?

A tremendous one! The organism's capacity to adapt to an ever-changing world was multiplied and sped up almost indefinitely. Our dependency from outer stimuli is the basis of our ability to learn and therefore to adjust ourselves apart from the classic biological laws of mutation and selection. But that is not all. When language was introduced step by step the learnt knowledge could be passed on to the next generations, even more so with the invention of writing. Recently the internet has created a pool of information accessible to everyone and unlimited in time and quantity.

If we consider all that, is it then still a surprise, that one result of the constant constructive processes in the brain is art? If constant production is the way the brain works, is it then not more surprising, that within all the creative overflow, still (most of the time) the outcome also includes an image of the outer world that sufficiently resembles it to assure survival in it.

It is exactly this constant production of content on the base of formerly stored experience dating back to the first prenatal impressions that is the root of creativity, be it manifested in dreams, in art, in hallucinations or in any other mode. Dreams, as Freud already suspected, most openly reveal and yet at the same time conceal the constructive process on the base of the formerly stored experience. Due to their free connective creation they seem to derive from a different world, but nevertheless they are based on the brain structure to the date they are generated.

Yet, interestingly enough, the integration of our current scientific knowledge of the brain's functioning into understanding the psyche is still massively suppressed by subconscious forces, especially irrational denial.

If we look at how the connective structure of our nerve cell system evolves, we easily observe two very simple and efficient rules: only where there is a stimulus, a structure is built and every existing structure tends to be used again, resulting in its reinforcement. It is like a street that is being built by driving on it, with a tendency to use it again, each time adding a new line.

Even though well proven and rather simple in nature, the consequences of this scientific basis are widely ignored. We learn about the impact of genes on who we are, but if you look at the facts their importance must be rather limited. We have about 22,500 genes, and 99.9 per cent of them are shared by all human beings. Nevertheless we show a huge variety of differences. So we have to look at genes as letters of an alphabet creating our features under the influence of the environment. It is the number and the order of them being activated that result in the language of who we are.

Similarly, crucial influences on the creation of our brain structures, to date, even though obvious, are completely ignored. If a connection between two brain cells depends on an external stimulus, all information in the brain has to be rooted in such stimuli until the complexity of the brain structure itself allows it to create its own inner stimuli – the starting point of abstract thinking. As a result, the first information to create our brain structure unquestionably is that of our prenatal life in the uterus.

Neurology offers a strange observation which is easily unveiled as a proof for this statement. The sensory representation of our bodily surface in the brain provides the evidence.

It is distorted. Not just are hands and lips bigger than in the actual body (because of their higher sensitivity more stimuli originate from them), but also lips and hands are in close proximity to each other, as are feet and genitalia, representing the position of the embryo and the fetus in the uterus, and thus, in opposition to Freud's concept, resulting in a rather profane explanation for foot fetishism. The way the stimuli arrive in the cortex creates its structure.

From this understanding, a new light is shed on our concept of paradise. We have all been there. Everyone's brain has a stored experience from a time when we never suffered from hunger, from thirst, from cold, from loneliness and, probably most importantly of all, from fear. Subconsciously, a force in us wants to return to this lost paradise – and for moments we actually can – for example, through meditation. Religion promises us that we will ultimately return. Indeed we do, yet unfortunately just for seconds and not for eternity.

An Alzheimer's patient loses his memory starting with his short-term memory. The earliest experiences remain stored in the memory the longest. A brain that is switched off in the process of dying therefore will lose the youngest stored information at first, then go backwards in time and in the final moment return to the earliest stored experiences, those from birth (people who survived having entered the process of dying describe the tunnel they entered) and from the life before birth – the completely sheltered paradise. Here we find a biological explanation for the supposed proof of its existence somewhere out there.

Immediately after birth the newborn starts to connect with the outer reality. The most determining factor in this conquest of the world is other people, as the brain reliably distinguishes between living and non-living objects, mainly through its mirroring cell system.

While in the beginning the other is only present in his role in the here and now, resulting in different concepts of partial object relations, the evolution of the capacity to store the image of the other over time is the first step towards an integration of the object.

Many of the earliest impressions which a brain perceives and which lead to its structure remain unknown and seem mysterious to us. In part this is because the first impressions are not verbally represented but do consist of physical sensations as well as of auditory and visual impressions. This is why they seem to be strange and foreign to our more or less adult way of thinking. At the same time, resistance towards the earliest memories may add to their repression. Maybe the early paradise was too good to be abandoned and its loss traumatic.

Yet it is the essence of these first perceived impressions which constitute what Freud named the unconscious. I am convinced that, looking at the biological build-up of the brain, no other explanation is possible but to understand the hidden traces of the unconscious in terms of the results of early experiences, mainly of those from inside the uterus as well as of those from inside the body of the growing embryo and fetus with needs and drives evolving within. Only if one claims that there is a force outside of our perceivable existence, like a god, can an alternative to this explanation be stated. Yet, even though common, there is no logical argument to support this alternative view of the world, which is something I will come back to.

For now let us look in detail at those influences building up the structure of the brain and thus being the roots of all its creations including art. Brain activity alone does not automatically result in the creation of art – this statement hardly needs an illustration. The knowledge which was created by a generation also needs to be passed on to the next to be accessible for transformation. Cold-blooded animals lack that ability – reptiles live without culture – which was only developed in warm-blooded creatures. Only their brains have special areas, which are sensitive to hormones like cortisol, which directly affect the activation of genes and therefore the development of certain traits, so that for example stress leads to an emotional reaction and a learning process which through changes in behavioural patterns then is passed on to the next generation. The capacity to adapt no longer depends on the rare chance of a beneficial mutation but is directly able to react to environmental changes.

Because of this enormous advance in adaptability, it is thanks to our brains that humans live in the most diverse surroundings, be it the jungle near the equator, the jungle of our cities, a remote island in the South Pacific, a high mountain region in the Himalayas or the icy world of the polar region. Even more so, people are able to adapt to situations that at first glance seem intolerable. They adjust their behavior to roles like that of torturer and prisoner (Zimbardo 2007), to that of slaughterer and martyr and tend to pass these perverted roles on to the next generations (which is one of the likely causes of the perpetuation of wars and homicide in some parts of the world).

The deep-rooted effects of transmitted thinking in the creation of societies and within it on to its art can lucidly be observed in Christian medieval art, which was inevitably dominated by religion. Medieval art had to serve Christianity. Tradition demanded this self limitation of content and style until the Renaissance revolutionised the perception of the world and liberated art from its tight boundaries.

Strangely enough in recent years Christian fundamentalists in Western societies intend to turn back the clock and reintroduce the dominance of religious belief on to their societies and cultures by implementing a so-called 'intelligent design' concept according to which there supposedly is scientific evidence of a planning power (a god) behind the evolving beauty of evolution.

In his recent book *The God Delusion*, neo-Darwinist author Richard Dawkins sums up contrary arguments. For example he states that the non-existence of a god cannot be proved, but neither can the non-existence of flying teapots or spaghetti monsters in space, claiming that it is not assumptions but scientific methods which define science. He also presents a list of the crimes that were committed in the name of faith to support his antireligious agenda. Furthermore he states that also without the creation of a fictional 'god' the world can be explained from a scientific point of view including the evolution of moral guidelines for human interactions. He considers religion a by-product of evolution which according to him is transmitted like a virus between people (Dawkins 2006).

In my view, Dawkins is right, yet his arguments are not new and often somewhat superficial. I doubt that the simplification he gives is able to explain the deep roots of human religious needs. I prefer to understand religion from a psychoanalytic point of view, linking it to the scientific evidence of our psychological development: once we become self perceptive during our early years of life, we start to ask existential questions. As the answers to those inevitably have to remain frustrating, we have created the phenomenon of a god to try to explain the unexplainable. Consecutively it is not a coincidence that the image of god evolved parallel to the evolution of the psyche and to the evolution of societies. The early gods were part of nature, explaining things mankind did not understand, like lightning and other natural phenomena. On the next level gods were transformed into a family which had obvious parallels to ordinary family life – or doesn't the Zeus family remind you of the Denver Clan?

Parallel to the process of psychological integration that any child goes through in normal development, the concepts of god also became more integrated, resulting in the single patrimonial figure of monotheism. Again, this new one-and-only god reflected the circumstances of its creators. The early Jewish god was as dangerous as was the everyday life of the Jewish people. Dawkins provides us with a shimmering caricature: 'The God of the Old Testament is arguably the most unpleasant character in all fiction: jealous and proud of it; a petty, unjust, unforgiving control-freak; a vindictive, bloodthirsty ethnic cleanser; a misogynistic, homophobic, racist, infanticidal, genocidal, filicidal, pestilential, megalomaniacal, sadomasochistic, capriciously malevolent bully' (Dawkins 2006: 191).

Later in the New Testament the god concept gained kindness and then was linked to a pantheistic experience of unity with the universe. At the same time, human emancipation allowed the option to fully abolish the need for a god, as Woody Allen put it in his film *Scoop*: 'I was born into the Hebrew tradition, but when I got older, I converted to Narcissism.'

Parallel to the psychodynamic development of each individual psyche (in societies where a high level of psychological integration has been reached) religion underwent fundamental changes as did the creation of art, both embedded in the progress of the joint wisdom of mankind which still is by no means evenly distributed to date (resulting in different concepts in different societies and even within them to explain the world).

But in addition to those learnt traditions that reflect themselves in art, are there also biologically inborn traits? Do we have artistic genes?

At this point it is certainly too early to answer this question. Also the existence of certain genes does not guarantee that they are necessarily activated. Yet, first results make it likely that there are some genetically determined inborn esthetic priorities all human beings share.

'Symmetry is beautiful.' Psychiatrist Manfred Spitzer tells us why:

> A symmetrical body is a healthy body. This rule not only is in force in humans, but also in animals. The reason for it is simple: infections, parasites, deformities and other illnesses of the body most commonly are not evenly affecting both arms, legs, eyes or ears. Illness, whatever its cause may be, therefore commonly leads to asymmetry.
>
> *(Spitzer 2007: 111)*

Cultural history, especially the abundant heritage of classical architecture, provides proof for this observation from the natural sciences. But still there are factors of beauty other than symmetry alone. One may relate to Freudian concepts of round forms or other characteristics of gender, or one may take a stroll into the shopping malls of our cities to observe how shiny objects attract the eyes of many of our fellow citizens – an effect which obviously is not limited to tribal cultures which gave away precious belongings in exchange for some glittering glass pearls. The mental root of this sometimes disadvantageous behaviour may likely be our dependency on water. Stone Age people had to search for water with their eyesight in the savannas they lived in (I mentioned the still fashionable Kalahari strategy earlier on) and were not like, for example, cats – able to sniff it. Similarly we are attracted by light, by the shining flames of the warming fire (which may be linked to the other humans likely to be encountered nearby), unless its dimensions are threatening (burning disasters).

Due to our social nature, our eyes tend to wander to any live object, the more human, the more attracting it is (not necessarily attractive). Other eyes are like magnets to our own visual system; our attention is immediately drawn towards them. Anything resembling a human being or another living object is at the center of our perception. This is even stronger in baby schemes. Inevitably we sympathise with anything that resembles an infant, yes, even with cars, although any rational thinking would contradict that. Car manufacturers like Volkswagen (Beetle) and Mazda without hesitation make use of our weak spots.

Key stimuli force their power upon us. We react like a warbler with a baby cuckoo in his nest – the bigger the stimulus the more we adore it. For the little warblers this means jumping over the edge of the nest (because the baby cuckoo's bill is brighter); for us the consequences vary. Usually they are linked to our basic needs, to food or sex. Art psychology has collected the evidence of those traps of our perception, which still await being likely linked to some genetic source some day ahead. We hardly resist oversized breasts, legs, eyes, or shoulders (Schuster 1997: 84–105).

We can assume that all these influences also find their way into art. Yet, the characteristics that decide whether we like a work of art or not, tend to be rather simple. In order to appeal to our taste, we need to recognise some familiar aspects in an artwork (which makes it dependent on our artistic education) and at the same time we want to be surprised by something new.

Interestingly enough, this 'law of art taste' has been proven in animals as well: 'A vervet monkey and a chimpanzee were given dies with colorful ornaments. They were allowed to choose some of them to play with. They preferred regular forms (avail or radial symmetry) over irregular ones. Also the color preference of the animals followed certain aesthetic criteria. After a few turns the monkeys and apes tended to switch their color of choice, as do people following the trends of fashion' (Schuster 1997: 81).

Taking this into account, it will no longer surprise us that some artists reach their fame long after their death. Van Gogh's stylistic inventions depended on the acceptance of impressionism to make their pictorial complexity understood and have their individual language of beauty integrated into the context of the art historical ideal.

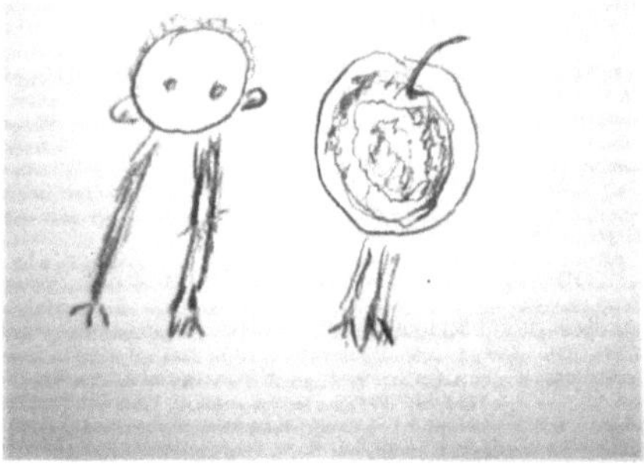

FIGURE 1.1

The fact that it is not culture alone that creates its impact on the oeuvre of an artist, also becomes visible in the following phenomenon: a brain has to mature, leading to stylistic phenomena at certain ages. When my 3-year-old daughter is drawing a person, she tends to focus on the head and then add legs and arms. The skipping of the trunk of the body is typical for her age. Curiously enough, this basic stylistic oddity is characteristic for the art of children aged between 2 and 4, but it is also found in tribal art as well as in the drawings of severely ill psychiatric patients, mainly those suffering from chronic schizophrenia and dementia (Figure 1.1).

Consequently we seem to be confronted with a minor observation leading to major assumptions. Obviously, the 'tadpole figure' person reflects a developmental stage of the psyche, respectively of the brain. Given the fact that early cultures produce the same stylistic features as young brains, there must be a parallel between the evolution of the psyche and the evolution of cultures. On the other hand the fact that psychiatric illness results in a transformation of thinking processes (visible in the drawing style) resembling those of children can be seen as evidence of the regressive potential of certain psychiatric conditions (Kraft 1997: 271–280).

Despite all these biological influences mentioned, art is not simply an inborn capacity. It has to be elaborated by the cultural tradition it is developed in. Yet even then it is not culture alone, but also the life experience of the artist apart from his or her artistic training, which leaves traces in art. Just on the basis of the given biology and the stored biographic experience, the artist starts to interact with culture.

How subtle the psychodynamic influence on an art can be, the oeuvres of several artists especially those from expressionism clearly reveal. As an example I give you two self portraits of the German expressionist Ernst Ludwig Kirchner from 1926 (Figure 1.2) and 1917 (Figure 1.3). The idealization in the latter and the devaluation in the earlier work represent the rapidly changing self perception of the artist due to a narcissistic personality disorder he suffered from and which was a major cause of his suicide in 1938 (Thomashoff 1997).

After thus having also focused on the various non-cultural aspects which influence the creation of a work of art, the last remaining question is: how does an artwork become recognised as such and how does it become integrated into the temple of appraised art history? The answer is: the same rules of interwoven

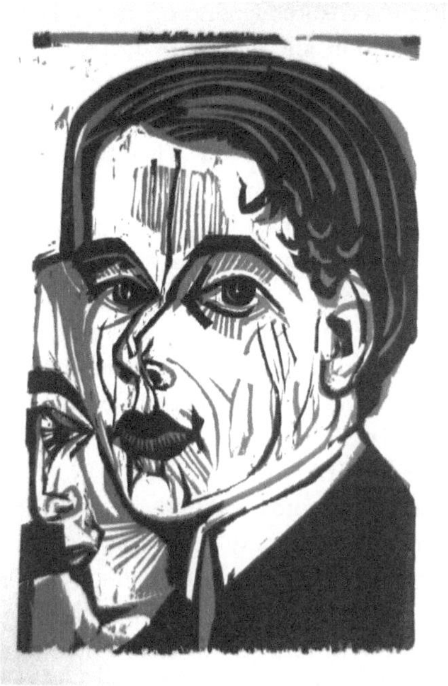

FIGURE 1.2

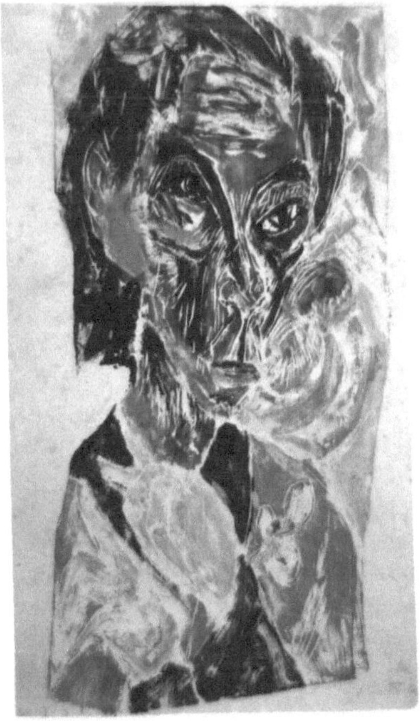

FIGURE 1.3

biological, psychodynamic and cultural influences that lead to an artwork's creation, also determine its interpretation, and with it, its attributed artistic value.

As an anecdote goes, Andy Warhol was once asked by a young artist, what he should do to get on the cover of Andy Warhol's influential art magazine, which would have made him an eminent success. The simple answer was: 'Sleep with me.' Usually it is not that easy to explain the course of an artistic career. More commonly it is a different strategy that opens the gate of the temple of fine arts. An artist whose individual psychodynamic connects with the stylistic tradition of the culture he is in creates an oeuvre in which his subjectivity reaches out to an inter-individual level and ascends to meaningfulness for society. This does not necessarily have to coincide with the artist's intention. For example the German Ludwig Meidner in 1912 painted apocalyptic scenarios of burning cities and people in a state of panic which were later interpreted as visionary intuitions of the upcoming disasters in the First World War.

Similarly, art brut was not accepted within the frame of the concepts of art until Dubuffet and others integrated its stylistic particularities into the field of the fine arts, resulting in a reciprocal acceptance of previously rejected artworks. They were not created within the tradition of the academic art, but the tradition changed and incorporated what had been brought to life outside of its former boundaries. Nowadays the drawings from the Prinzhorn Collection, the paintings of Aloise and many more have entered museums and the art market on an equal level as others. Nevertheless these evolutions of traditions do neither progress evenly within a society nor between different societies. Another anecdote may reveal this: a bathtub which had been filled with grease and other things by Joseph Beuys was first used to cool beer and then laboriously cleaned by an eager cleaning woman who thus faced charges of destroying a highly valuable work of art.

References

Andreasen, N.C. and Black, D.W. (2001) *Introductory Textbook of Psychiatry* (3rd edition), Washington D.C.: American Psychiatric Publishing.

Dawkins, R. (2006) *The God Delusion*, Boston: Houghton Miflin.

Hacker, F. (1971) *Aggression: Die Brutalisierung der Modernen Welt. [Aggression: The Brutalization of the Modern World]*, Wien: Molden, 1971.

Kraft, H. (1997) 'Die Kopffüßler [Tadpole Figure People]' in: I. Brugger, P. Gorsen, and K.A. Schröder: *Kunst und Wahn [Art and Madness]*, Exhibition Catalagoue at the Kunstforum Wien, Köln: Dumont.

Schuster, M. (1997) *Wodurch Bilder Wirken [How Images Work]* (3rd edition), Köln: Dumont.

Spitzer, M. (2007) *Vom Sinn des Lebens [On the Meaning of Life]*, Stuttgart: Schattauer.

Thomashoff, H.-O. (1997) *Die Suizidalität in Leben und Werk Ernst Ludwig Kirchner [Suicidality in the Life and Work of Ernst Ludwig Kirchner]*, Ph.D. dissertation, University of Hamburg.

Zimbardo, P. (2007) *The Lucifer Effect*, New York: Random House.

2

NORM(S) AND THE FUNCTION OF OUTSIDER ART

Ekaterina Sukhanova

Art perception relies on a dialogical communication between the artist, the audience, and the cultural context, which allows for new interpretations to be made and new meanings to be generated. Inherent in all artistic activity, these dialogical mechanisms become particularly striking in outsider art and can serve as a basis for fighting stigma. All artistic creation is a bridge to the social: artworks can exist only among other artworks and must be preceded by them. 'An isolated text is incapable of generating meanings; like any dynamic generating system, a text requires input of outside information, which in this case implies an interaction with other texts and cultural environments' (Lotman 1992: 146–147).

The aesthetic value of an artwork does not depend on the fulfilment of the norm. In non-artistic communication it is not the language but its content that carries information: we do not pay attention to the shade of red used on a stop sign. While this aspect of communication remains present in art, it is not exclusive nor is it necessarily the primary one. Although in a non-artistic communication it is precisely the adherence to the rules that ensures adequate transmittal of a message, in a work of art this proves insufficient, and often even detrimental. Simple adherence to a set of rules will not yet create aesthetic value. 'If we dealt only with a strict system of rules, each new work would represent an exact copy of a previous one, redundancy would prevail over entropy and the artwork would lose its informational value' (Lotman 1998: 276). Kitsch is an example of artwork that copies existing models unquestioningly, without adding a meaningful change that could alter the interpretation.

If mere adherence to the norm does not yet creative artistic value, neither does the complete destruction of the norm. The long-standing popular misconception of outsider art, going back to Jean Dubuffet's first coinage of 'art brut' (which is still being most commonly rendered in English as 'outsider art', in spite of many attempts to find a less value-laden term), presents outsider art as being free from –

or unsullied by – existing conventions, social or aesthetical. This romanticised notion of the outsider artist as the modern-day 'noble savage' is easily challenged in an age when access to the Internet is widespread and long-term institutional isolation is rare. More importantly, this contradicts the nature of artwork as a semiotic structure.

Indeed, art without any cultural or social context is impossible. Limitless choices, absence of any rules, and absolute freedom from any imposed limits are not the ideal state, but the death of communication: this is why a reader facing a text produced in an unfamiliar writing system perceives it as a random collection of symbols. All art represents a dynamic relationship between following an existing aesthetical norm and deviating from it. At a deeper level of analysis, a work of art exists at the intersection of many concurrently active aesthetic norms. The unique nature of art consists in establishing relations among a wide variety of languages and codes present in a culture and transforming these languages from a tool into an object of their work.

Art production allows a maximum freedom of choice for the individual artist while at the same time providing a connection to existing rules, conventions and structures. The greater the number of potential choices available to the artist, the more valuable will be the information represented by a particular choice. The audience's assumptions of the author's intention and accountability play a particularly big role in the interpretation of outsider art. The greater the awareness of an existing artistic convention to which the new work is responding, the more acute is the audience's perception of the unique qualities of this work. The individual and the universal are no longer isolated but, on the contrary, require each other.

In the words of Joseph Brodsky, a Nobel Prize Laureate for Literature, 'the more substantial an individual's aesthetic experience is ... the freer ... he is' (Brodsky 1995: 49–50). This is even more true in the case of patients struggling with mental illness, who often find themselves constrained both by the reality of their medical condition and by the social stigma surrounding it. To help visualise the potential of art for combating stigma and promoting inclusion, we will turn to the conceptual model of 'vicious circles' of stigmatisation as formulated by Sartorius (Sartorius 2000). According to this concept, a marker that allows a person to be identified with it can be loaded with negative contents by association with existing stereotypes and prejudices. Once a marker is negatively loaded, it becomes stigma and the individual who bears it will inevitably be stigmatised. The experience of discrimination leads to impaired functioning and reinforces stigma, establishing a vicious circle.

Art can counteract stigma by weakening or breaking this vicious cycle in two parts. First, the dialectical mechanisms of art may be built upon in order to preventing a marker from becoming associated with stigma. Stigmatisation has at its root the objectification of the other – that is, denying him or her the right to be an independent agent in the communication process. It also involves rejection of any new information that may lead to altering existing constructs. In sum, stigmatisation is a breakdown of communication. Art affords us an alternative: a model of dialogue in which the other is accepted as an equal partner in the communication process. 'I cannot become myself without the other; I must find myself in the other, finding the other in me (in mutual reflection and perception)' (Bakhtin, quoted in Todorov, 1984: 96).

Further, art allows for critical distance, retrospection, and vast opportunities for individual choice, and thus may be conducive to an improved self-image and self-esteem. In producing art, the artist interacts with his or her internalised objects. The creative act can become a therapeutic tool, extending from verbal experiences into non-verbal and preverbal experiences across all stages of psychological development: while providing a path for a validation of an artist's own experience, the creative act is also intrinsically linked to abstraction, or the ability to see the universal in the individual. Twentieth-century critical theory made much of art's ability to show things anew for the reader or viewer, be it Brecht's 'alienation' (*Verfremdungseffekt*) or Shklovsky's 'estrangement' (*ostranenie*), but it was Bakhtin who focused specifically on the critical distance that is created between the artist and his or her immediate experience. This phenomenon, for which Bakhtin coined the term of 'being outside,' is sometimes translated as 'outsidedness' or 'exotopy' (*vnenakhodimost*). After the initial fusional stage where the artist and the character merge, the artist has to disengage from the character's affective state and establish a boundary in order to complete the creative work: 'Aesthetic activity begins properly only when one returns into oneself at one's place, outside of the one suffering' (op. cit.: 99). For Bakhtin, this mental distancing is a necessary prerequisite for artistic expression. Regardless of whether a narrative character is meant to be purely autobiographical (or the visual artwork is meant as a self-portrait) – although this is very common in outsider art – the artist has to transcend self-identification with the created image and assume an external point of view. The creative process acquires therapeutic properties as it aids the artist to cease being engulfed by emotions and start developing an integrated identity. Capitalising on the intrinsic properties of the artistic process reaffirms the artist's dignity and helps counteract not only social stigma, but self-stigmatisation as well: 'The patient's particularized, broken, fragmented self must fit into a more manageable flow. Then, the patient eases his/her way into a slow process of identity change.... Self-transformation is the objective of all art, and the [patient] artists ... no less than others' (Marton 2002: 15).

Aesthetic function arises at the intersection of highly individual activities and established cultural codes and structures. Any art object is saturated with values and must be analysed in relation to its surrounding society in order to understand how it is perceived. It is the human collective in a given time and place that may or may not perceive the aesthetic function as the dominating one (for example, objects that had practical or religious significance at the time of their creation may be perceived primarily as artistic objects today). The same artistic object might have multiple functions, ranging from the aesthetic to the therapeutic, social and ceremonial, which might vary both diachronically and synchronically: 'Stabilizing the aesthetic function is a matter for the collective and is a component in the relationship between the human collective and the world' (Mukařovský 1970: 18). The more the viewers are aware of an existing cultural convention to which artwork is responding, the stronger they perceive the individuality and uniqueness of the new creative approach.

No longer isolated, the individual and the universal require each other in art. The unique nature of art consists in establishing relations among a wide variety of languages and codes present in a culture and transforming these languages from a tool into an object of their work. The interaction between norm and innovation functions as a mechanism generating new messages, or meanings. This dynamic relation between autonomy and connectedness underpinning the processes of art creation and perception is akin to Ricoeur's dialectic notion of identity. Ricoeur sees the notion of 'selfhood' (*soi-même*) as created through a dynamic mediation between the two poles of personal identity, the pole of 'sameness', (*la mêmeté*), understood as a set of innate or acquired attitudes and capacities that enables a spatio-temporal coherence, and the pole of 'self-sameness' (*la laipséité*), understood as the most concrete and particular core of a subject that enables initiation of new things (Ricoeur 1990: 8).

The creative act can therefore be considered as unconscious repairing of the body ego, conducive to increased individual psychological stability (feeling connected to oneself) and collective inclusion (the capacity to be connected to others). Erikson (1980) also suggests that the individual gains a 'sense of reality from the awareness that his individual way of mustering experience, his ego synthesis is a successful variant of a group identity', and this is understood as conferring 'status and stature' on the individual (Erikson 1980: 21–22). Connecting spectators to meaning just as it connects the authors to collectivity, art fosters cooperative communication in which dignity and individuality of a mental health patient may be reaffirmed.

One of the most common genres in outsider art across cultures and time periods is the self-portrait and the portrait in general. The portrait relies on body image as a frame of reference for all cognitive functions and a key element in emotional functioning. Oscillating between a metonymical representation of a human being and a projection of certain cultural and social assumptions, the portrait has been referred to as 'the most philosophical painting genre. It is built on the juxtaposition of that which human beings are and that which they ought to be' (Lotman 1998: 514). Being situated between semantic oppositions, portraits have a particularly high communicative intensity. 'A portrait is akin to a double mirror: through it, art is reflected in life and life is reflected in art. It is not only the reflections but also the realities which switch places' (Lotman 1998: 51). The borderline between the reflected and the reflection is not a fixed one: a binary unit is transformed to a multidimensional construction. The reconstruction of the body image in portraiture may be an anchorage point in allowing the artist to perceive heterogeneity as empowerment.

Art has the capacity of changing the structural self-orientation not only of the artist, but also of the viewer and, over time, the larger sociocultural context as well.

'In the realm of culture, outsidedness is a most powerful factor in understanding. It is only in the eyes of another culture that foreign culture reveals itself fully and profoundly (but not maximally fully, because there will be cultures that see and understand even more)' (Bakthin 1990: 7). To continue evolving, any living culture relies on constant exchange between the peripheral and mainstream, archaic and innovative, 'insider' and 'outsider' cultural production, a dynamic which parallels the construction of an individual's notion of self through interaction with cultural others. Asymmetry and ongoing productive exchange between central and peripheral realms is more than simply a desirable change of pace: it is the very mechanism that assures the continuation of a semiotic system. When this dynamic is interrupted, e.g. in isolated or totalitarian societies, the resulting loss of intersubjectivity leads to cultural stagnation that is inevitably fraught with decline and obliteration. Just as an individual deprived of outside stimuli, a culture deprived of exchange with other cultures is at a risk of becoming dysfunctional. Culture as such is polyglossal.

Historically, scholarly interest in outsider art first arose out of a specific clinical task, using patient art to confirm a mental health diagnosis. The use of patient art is no longer limited to differential diagnostics, however. Because all artistic activity is also a communicative act, working with patient art may aid the clinician to gain a better understanding of the preserved aspects of a patient's personality, beyond the pathological syndromes, and build a better rapport. In this way, art is a resource for the clinician in effective planning of specific medical and social rehabilitation strategies. At the community level, public exhibitions of psychiatric art, as promoted by the World Psychiatric Association and its Section on Art and Psychiatry, may also be an effective tool in anti-stigma campaigns. These exhibits serve a greater purpose than merely disrupting the historic association between mental health and art in institutional space: they counteract negative social stereotypes of mental illness as well as undermining the cultural mechanisms for stigma. For many of the artists, allowing their work to be seen might effectively be the only meaningful form of communication with other individuals or with the outside world at large. The process of participating in a creative act already engages artists in a conversation, and many are proud to have their art exhibited and their message find resonance with others. This communicative value of art does not hinge on any formal official recognition or even on an opportunity to socialise with peers; although these positive experiences are desirable, their absence does not yet efface the dialogical dynamics.

Stigmatisation has at its root the turning of the other into an object, effectively denying to him or her the right to be an independent active partner in the communication process. The psychological basis of stigma is the destruction of communication. Art, relying on the opposite mechanism, may be instrumental in changing the context in which mental illness is experienced, thereby reducing stigma and promoting reintegration. With its powerful potential for changing both the self-regard of the artist and the externally imposed identity, 'art is the anti-destiny,' to use an expression of André Malraux (1951: 637). The dialogical potential of art allows us to better grasp the origins of vulnerability as well as the cognitive, emotional and behavioural issues critical to improving the experience of self.

References

Bakhtin, M. [M. Holquist and V. Liapunov, eds] (1990) *Art and Answerability: Early Philosophical Essays by M.M. Bakhtin*, Austin, TX: University of Texas Press.

Brodsky, J. (1995) *On Grief and Reason*, New York: Farrar, Straus & Giroux.

Davies, B. (1991) 'The concept of agency: a feminist poststructuralist analysis', *Social Analysis*, 30: 42–53.

Erikson, E.H. (1968) *Identity: Youth And Crisis*, London: Faber.

Erikson, E.H. (1980) *Identity and the Life Cycle*, New York: Norton and Company, Inc.

Lotman, Yu (1992) *Izbrannye Stat'i* [*Selected Articles*], vol. 1, Tallinn: Alexandra.

Lotman, Yu (1998) *Ob Iskusstve* [*On Art*], St. Petersburg: Iskusstvo-SPb.

Malraux, A. (1951) 'Les voix du silence', in: *La Monnaie de l'Absolu (Essais De Psychologie De L'Art)*, Paris: Gallimard.

Marton, J. (ed.) (2002) *Journey of Hope*, New York: Bristoll-Myer Squibb Co & Todd Street Productions and Creedmor Psychiatric Center.

Mukařovský, J. (1970) *Aesthetic Function, Norm and Value as Social Facts* (trans. Mark E. Suino), Ann Arbor: University of Michigan Press.

Ricoeur, P. (1990) *Soi-Même Comme un Autre*, Paris: Editions du Seuil.

Sartorius, N. (2000) 'Breaking the vicious circle', *Mental Health and Learning Disabilities Care*, 4: 80.

Sukhanova, E. (2013) 'Psychiatry in art: A means for healing and fighting stigma': *Psychiatric Times*, March 2013: 22, 24.

Themersma, D. (1989) *Body Schema and Body Image. An Interdisciplinary and Philosophical Study*, Amsterdam: Swets & Zeitlinger.

Thomashoff, H.-O. (ed.) (2002) *Human Art Project*, Stuttgart: Schattauer.

Thomashoff, H.-O. and Sukhanova, E. (eds) (2008) *The Person in Art: Conceptual and Pictorial Frames on Outsider Art*, New York: Nova Science Publishers.

Todorov, T. (1984) *Mikhail Bakhtin: The Dialogical Principle* (trans. Wlad Godzich), Minneapolis, MN: University of Minnesota Press.

3

BODY AND IDENTITY

Objects of redemption in today's unrest

Angélique Christaki

Where the body comes from

A series of enthusiastic and impassionate claims about the body, its rights and safety cast light on the singular coordinates that we may use to try and think, in today's society, about the foundations of the question of the human body and its destiny.

To my mind, these claims reflect an obstruction in the possibility of thinking about what founds a body for a subject, that is to say of thinking about the body as a site of otherness *par excellence*. The sliding from the position of the body as otherness towards its position as a living substance, identified through its genetic identity, are signs of the impoverishment of the current debate on the body.

This includes, for example, the NeuroSpin project, a medical imaging platform, full of new energy and seeking answers to one of the greatest human mysteries: 'How are thoughts created?'[1]

The platform presents a research project into the origin of thought, which uses new technological methods to map the mythical moment in which thought becomes anchored in the body. From this perspective, the researchers are planning to render visible and thus potentially controllable the umbilical cord of what can be represented and the origin of what is human. More specifically, using positive scientific proof, they are trying to grasp and identify the mythic primal moment when a living body becomes a human body, a speaking and desiring being.

However, such promise merely echoes a double confusion. On the one hand, the confusion between the status of the origin and that of the beginning, and on the other hand the confusion between the status of the living body and that of a human body as a body of speech and a libidinal body.

This double confusion forgets what the psychoanalytic clinic continuously argues, when it situates the origin of the human in an impossible-to-demonstrate and ultimately never-quite-completed movement, marked by the limits of our mortal and sexual destiny. In addition, this movement can only be understood based on, firstly, the relationship to otherness constituted by the relationship to the body, and secondly, the inscription of the limits to seeing and knowing.

Lifting the veil: a systematic injunction

This attempt to identify the mythical primal moment represents a concern that is not altogether recent. The human desire to see behind all limits is indeed a very old dream. We may recall the biblical story of Salome, who, when dancing in front of Herod, lifts her veils one by one until the last seventh veil; when she appears naked in front of the King, he orders her to remove the next veil.

Today, it is no longer the myth that functions as a support to our preoccupation with the origin, but science: science and technology lend support to the human dream of being able to see what is behind the last veil – to see inside the human body.

Throughout human history, the interior of the human body had always been a space impenetrable to the human gaze. While the Ancient Greeks forbade all dissection of corpses, the only exception being the remains of traitors, the Egyptians practiced dissection on the living bodies of criminals. It was not until the sixteenth century that Vesalius in Padua began to officially open human corpses and explore the interior of the human body, thus endowing the act with a scientific purpose.[2] Nonetheless, even though dissections were attended by large crowds, it was the painter Jan Joest van Kalkar, a student of Titian, whose pencil copied the images of the dissected corpse, representing the inside of the body and revealing to the viewer a category of the real, previously inaccessible to the eye. In this way, the stroke of the pen of Master Van Kalkar becomes a gesture to sustain the function of the seventh veil, going against the direction of Vesalius's scalpel.

Today, the formidable and undeniable progress of science and medicine has 'democratised' the access to the inside of the body.[3]

The question that I have been led to ask myself, based on my clinical practice, is the following: what effects does this simplified and immediate access inside the body have on the level of the structuring of body image – an image conditioning our relationship to the world?

Specifically, what are the consequences, both subjective and collective, of this generalised access to what had previously always been situated on the level of the forbidden, of horror, and the sacred?

These problems provoke an ethical, social and legal reflection, which is evidenced by, on the one hand, the current debate on bioethics and the use of living materials as separate from what makes us human beings, i.e. our identity and our limits, and, on the other hand, the debate on biometrics, which establishes the identity signature based on the irrefutable trace of the genetic signature, i.e. on what is 'identical' rather than 'other'.[4]

The reference to identity does not simply have to do with the question 'who am I?', but also 'who am I for the other?' In this way, understanding identity in the social space based on the idea of the identical,[5] from anatomical matter to biological identity, means negating the status of the body as otherness and reducing the intimacy of the symbolic, genealogical link to its merely genetic base.

Grounding identity in a reference to the image and the visible, referring it to a biological substance identical to its own matter, means removing the intimacy of the symbolic link to the body and to the other, a link that can transform matter into a space of subjectivity.

Place of burial, place of distraction

It is also clear that in our contemporary societies, intimacy is being systematically eradicated. This eradication jeopardises the possibility of accidents or encounters in the individual's life being transformed into psychic events. Obstructing such elaboration constitutes a damage to human temporality, which in turn compromises the possibility of elaborating individual loss and pain, in the tissue of the subject's psychic life, into a space of intimacy, i.e. a place of burial of subjective losses that can be elaborated as such by the work of mourning.

As a result, the current malaise in our civilisation, in terms of the imperative of transparency, can be considered as a generalised attempt to transform the social bond into a bond of distraction and forgetting, that is to say into a bond which no longer allows for life events to be remembered and historicised as psychic events. However, a bond that impedes memory prevents the inscription of the tragic condition of existence, which ultimately constitutes the foundation of our identity as speaking beings.

In our culture, this tragic condition[6] gradually loses its space of elaboration, while the place that seems to be dedicated to it is that of distraction.

Often it is the artists whose work – sometimes provocative, at other times enigmatic or funny – attracts the gaze of our contemporaries to the barbarism inherent in all cultural progress.

In this respect, Von Hagens's work is exemplary. The artist has invented an original technique, a procedure of preserving fresh corpses through the method of 'plastination'. He has then exhibited them in arrangements suggesting ordinary everyday activities, sports, etc. Certain bodies have been opened, exposing their equally plastinated insides to the spectator's gaze, so that he or she can contemplate the smallest details of muscular striations, the innervation of the organ tissue and even the tumour which caused the individual's death.

However, the exhibited corpses have lost their status as human remains; they are now only identical to the laminated flesh of indifferent identity. In other words, these are not corpses that are meant to be buried and that are meant to reach the rank of ancestors via the symbolic gesture of burial and the inscription of a name on a tombstone.

We should note that it is a big step to take from the time of Sophocles's Antigone to the use of solid bodies for aesthetic purposes and sensual enjoyment.

In addition, the success of the exhibition, which could be questioned as a social symptom, has also been remarkable: 780,000 visitors in Mannheim, where the exhibit had to remain open 24 hours a day in order to satisfy the demand of the public; two and a half million visitors in Tokyo, and an unprecedented success in Vienna.[7]

The show, essentially sustained by a scopic jouissance that transforms death into a spectacle and thus denies the human corpse the humanising gesture of a proper burial, has clearly been very popular. If we consider that the advent of humanity happens through this very same gesture of burial, what damage to the human and to the human condition is the current backtracking in the cultural progress going to cause?

Let us take another example from the domain of art. Hiding things in the shade, removing them from the field of the visible: that is what inspires the work of Renaud Auguste Dormeil. In 2001, the artist created a device called 'Counter-Project Panopticon'. It consists of a racing bicycle, which allows the individual to travel from one place to another without being visible from a plane, a helicopter, a satellite, i.e. without being identifiable by a vertical gaze. Concretely, the object includes several reflective panels: thanks to a carefully orchestrated game of mirrors, these panels reflect an image that makes the device invisible.[8]

In other words, the artist hides the cyclist and his bicycle from direct view, we could say sheltering them from the contemporary obligation of absolute transparency, of a visibility without a shadow, an image of a human universe that offers no shelter to the intimate.

It should also be noted that this reflection is not meant to be part of an ideology of decline but is intended to think about the singularity of a characteristic of our time – the obligation of transparency – and to subject it to the community of those whose work concerns the human, while leaving these questions intentionally open.

Notes

1 Cited by Gérard Wajcman (2010) in *L'Œil Absolu*, Paris: Denoël: p. 29.

2 Vesalius's *De Humantis Corporis Fabrica* ['On the Fabric of the Human Body'] is the most important anatomical treatise since Galen and the first illustrated work of anatomy.

3 Japanese researchers from the Institute of Marine Biology at the University of Hiroshima, who were trying to study the inside of the body of a frog, without performing any incisions, have succeeded in making the frog's skin transparent. G. Wajcman uses the following fitting expression: 'The little animal alone embodies the apocalypse of the visible'. (In *L'Œil Absolu*, op. cit., p. 22)

4 This is precisely the comment made by Deleuze (2003), when he designates the contemporary society as a society of control. The subjects submit themselves to surveillance, no longer having need for an intermediary. From the injunction to visibility referred to by Foucault to Deleuze's imperative of seeing/being seen, subjects become permanent agents of the construction of their own panoptical surveillance. On this topic, I refer the reader to Deleuze's text 'Postscript on the societies of control' in *Negotiations*.

5 Writing in 2004, Jean Baudrillard makes the following critical and incisive remark: 'Being unable to conceive that identity has never existed and that it is merely something we play-act, we continue to feed this subjective illusion to the point of exhaustion. We wear ourselves out feeding this ghost of a representation of ourselves' (*The Intelligence of Evil and the Lucidity Pact*, p. 57, trans. Chris Turner). Baudrillard argues that in the

illusion that in order to exist, we need the idea of identity rather than otherness, is one of the characteristics of our times.

6 A. Christaki, 'Quand Zeus joue aux dés il gagne toujours', *Recherches Psychanalytiques*, online, 2010.

7 C. Melman, 'Enfin une jouissance nouvelle, la nécroscopie', in *L'Homme sans Gravité*, Paris : Denoël, 2005.

8 Cited in *L'Œil Absolu*, op. cit., p. 186.

References

Arasse, D. (1996). *Le Détail, Pour une Histoire Rapprochée de la Peinture*, Paris: Flammarion.

Baudrillard, J. (2004). *Le Pacte de Lucidité ou l'Intelligence du Mal*, Paris: Galilée.

Capgras, J. and Reboul-Lachaux, J. (1923). 'L'illusion des sosies dans un délire systématisé chronique', in *Bull. Soc. Clin. Ment.*, XI.

Capgras, J. and Carette, P. (1924). 'I'illusion des sosies et complexe d'Œdipe', in *Annales Méd-Psych*, 12(2).

Christaki, A. (2010). 'Quand Zeus joue aux dés il gagne toujours', *Recherches Psychanalytiques*, 1(9): 108–112

Deleuze, G. ([1991] 2003). *Pourparleurs*, Paris: Éditions de Minuit.

Freud, S. (1885). *L'Inquiétante Étrangeté et Autres Essais*, Paris: Gallimard.

Melman, C. (2005). *L'Homme sans Gravité*, Paris: Denoël.

Wajcman, G. (2010). *L'Œil Absolu*, Paris: Denoël.

4

CONTEMPORARY BODY

Medicine to modern art

Rémy Potier

The position of medicine today

Today's medicine is technoscientific. I would like to show that this fact engenders a new representation of the body in the social field, including a new relationship of the subject to his own body. A normalising process can be identified not only in the area of healthcare, but also on the anthropological level. Highlighting this dimension reveals the importance of an interdisciplinary perspective when studying medicine and more specifically medical imaging. The medical image of the body is an image of the internal body, a body that is constructed, one that is 'other' and is continuously perceived as foreign. This body only comes into existence thanks to technologies of virtualisation, and thanks to considerable computing power. The subject is confronted with an experience of immersion. The image represents the body, yet it is a body produced *for* medical purposes and only legible through medicine's own means. This is reflected in the social field on two levels. Firstly, at the level of the vocabulary related to the body, which becomes saturated with medical terms. Secondly, in what concerns the question of 'transference,' in the psychoanalytic sense of the term, as physicians encounter it today.

The language of medicine, its discourse, inevitably plays an important role in the way today's representations of the body are constructed. In present-day medical procedures, CT scanning, ultrasound and MRI have become as commonplace as traditional X-ray scanning. 'My doctor was not worried about my scan', 'My ultrasound was strange' – these are just two examples of what patients say, examples which can illustrate the implication of the medical imaging technology in contemporary common parlance. This linguistic development should surprise us, in that it is the result of an unconscious formation based on personal experiences of different bodily encounters with these technologies, more often than not in a situation where the subject knows nothing of their real functioning and implications. In this type of speech, the body is seen through what exposes it – the organ is replaced by the investigative technology and lived experience is condensed into a *high-tech* magical formula. We can no longer speak about our body and its functioning without having recourse to medical vocabulary. The body is to us an ensemble of organs, which are the site of physiological and biochemical processes. Therefore, we designate and localise our illnesses according to medical geography and terminology, even if these do not exactly follow the official nomenclature.

Medical knowledge feeds into language and representation, yet to patients it remains largely impenetrable. Clearly, these borrowed words orient our body representation and experience, and the technical vocabulary we use allows us to turn our body into an external object we can keep, at least minimally, at a distance, thus warding off the concerns and worries it may be causing us. However, something remains outside representation and this remainder returns to us. Psychoanalytic inquiry is interested precisely in this returning reminder. For medical practitioners, relating to a body as a purely external object has become a matter of course. The specificity of contemporary medical knowledge, in addition to the technical vocabulary we borrow from it, lies in the fact that the reconstructed body imposes itself on us as a supposed objectivity, despite being in reality a construction, from which we should – though it is not always possible – maintain some distance. Nonetheless, for the patient, this body-object does not represent the whole truth of his illness.

The demands of patients and the transference[1] to the medical body must be understood in this context. However, today's religiosity is situated at the level of technological processes. Encouraged by the media, the amazed and fascinated society considers 'medical progress' to be practically limitless. Television series such as *ER*, *Grey's Anatomy* or *House* have become a window onto the latest advances in medical technology; their scripts are co-written by medical practitioners and promote the use of medical terms. The viewer's incomprehension stimulates the heroic identification with the medical staff. If science is identified with progress, medicine is also thought to be able to produce miracles and this message constitutes its religiosity. Each new advance seems to efface the traces of the preceding one; however, medical progress is in fact achieved against a background haunted by the anxiety of death, which must constantly be warded off and silenced. Thus we see a number of contradictory visions clashing against each other. The physician's perspective on his own science is never identical to the patient's view of his illness and the words the latter learns from the media only accentuate the gap between these two perspectives, thus further complicating their encounter.

The movement from the reality of the body into the virtuality of the parametric standards of images and figures, of this truly new reality, draws the consciousness of the body towards the outside. Techno-scientific medicine replaces subjectivity with medical science, which can, for better or worse, serve as the body's new identity. In the sense of a simple increase in possibilities, the new advances of psychopharmacology, electric interference or brain computing no longer make any difference between one's own body, neurotransmitters and external organs.

Physicians tell us that a patient's condition may worsen simply because he is told about an existing risk of illness or because the doctors are unable to determine the cause of his malady; at other times, a condition can improve by virtue of the patient having received favourable results. We are no longer able to discern the truth about our bodies. On the collective level, this loss of individual trust in the signals of one's own body only becomes accentuated. The truth of the body is seen as residing in the hands of the medical practitioner. Medical progress therefore results in the creation of a new and increasingly efficient real, while disregarding the fact that the human being too is being transformed.

This article will try to show *what happens in the encounter with the imagery of the internal body*, effects which the work of artists who use medical imaging techniques in their creative process brings into clearer focus.

Drawing back the veil on the body, from imaging to art

In trying to understand the subject's encounter with medical imaging, modern art offers us an extremely useful perspective. I would like to begin by presenting the work of Mona Hatoum. We find that many contemporary artists have been inspired by medical technologies; the last decade of the twentieth century in particular experienced a new wave of *body art*. As an example of this work, I would like to discuss Hatoum's piece *Foreign Body* (1994).

Hatoum's work is a video installation showing endoscopic images of the interior of the artist's own body. My inquiry focuses on the fantasmatic logic it articulates as a correlate of the discourse and equipment produced by scientific technology. I argue that the artist depicts this logic in order to transmit her own gaze on the object. The artist's gaze unfolds in the device, reflecting something of the discontents of the modern perspective on the body.

As part of the *body art* tradition, Mona Hatoum's work has always foregrounded the body; camera surveillance has been another of her recurring themes. In *Don't Smile, You're on Camera*, a live performance which took place in 1980, the public was filmed and the images mixed with other visual elements, for example juxtaposing a well-dressed spectator with a nude image or an X-ray scan. When projected on screen, these images gave the impression of the camera's gaze slipping both under the person's clothes and under his skin. This staging of the problem of voyeurism gives the spectator a chance to experience the switch between voyeurism and exhibitionism. The artist therefore succeeds in producing a kind of metonymy of the effect experienced by the modern subject, who seems destined to become completely immersed in the world of images. However, this voyeurism is performed by the camera eye, which in Hatoum's 1994 piece *Foreign Body* in fact penetrates the body. This invasive gaze is simultaneously fascinating and terrifying, indeed violent. The work seems to imply both a fascination with the unknown parts of the body and a critique of the appropriative imaging technology, thus in fact restoring its anxiety-producing dimension.

Foreign Body consists of a type of cabin, which we can enter in order to see and feel the artwork. On the floor of the cabin there is a round screen, where we see the projection of enlarged footage of the surface and the interior of the artist's body.[2] We can follow the endoscopic camera as it brushes against the artist's skin and penetrates through its orifices, such as the anus and the vagina, in order to film the body's insides. The movements of the camera are accompanied by the amplified noise of the artist's breathing and heartbeat: when the camera remains outside the body, we hear the sound of breathing; when it enters inside, we hear the sound of a heartbeat. The relatively small cabin and the necessity of standing directly on the screen give the spectator a feeling of being absorbed *inside* the artist's body. He is captured in a 'strangely intimate circle' between the body's interior and exterior.

Mona Hatoum participated in the production of this video by remaining awake and conscious during a medical exam. The work unveils before us the most intimate areas of her body, the access to which is in principle solely reserved to the medical gaze as an organ of control. This is the first meaning of the work's title, which designates the camera as the extension of the scientific gaze, as an external element penetrating the patient's body, appropriating it and reporting on it through deconstructed images. To the extent that the examined body, in spite of its familiarity, becomes itself foreign, unrecognizable to the individual to whom it belongs – leaving aside the fact that medical imagery can sometimes reveal an anomaly unsuspected by the subject, thus adding to the feeling of alienation towards one's own body. In addition, the expression *Foreign Body* also refers to the spectator's position within the framework of the installation. In deciding to enter the structure that houses the endoscopic video, the spectator becomes involved with an unknown body, which he is invited to explore through the larger-than-life images, amplifying the effect of being immersed in another territory, delimited by the circular architecture. Whether the spectator bypasses the image by walking alongside the inner walls of the structure surrounding the video, or whether he decides to cross the projection screen diagonally, he cannot avoid a confrontation with a body shown in its most biological aspects.

The type of structure designed by the artist to contain the endoscopic video has a determining effect on the reception of the work by the spectator: the relatively small form of the cylinder – accessible only through two narrow doors – suggests a private space with limited access. This feeling is accentuated by the almost complete darkness of the surroundings (the video images are the only source of light in the installation). Then, once the spectator has entered the structure, the extremely intimate nature of the projected images inevitably puts him in the position of a voyeur. Moreover, *Foreign Body* also refers to the notion of surveillance and the correlation between the gaze and power, a notion largely developed by Foucault. Indeed, the encounter within this architectural space, between the artist's body and the spectator's gaze, functions as a spatial reconstruction of the power exercised by the medical institution through its scientific gaze, which is directed to the vulnerable body of the patient.

Foreign Body is not one's own body; it is not my body but the body of an other. Yet the body shown on the screen is no longer completely familiar even to the artist herself. The intervention of a foreign entity in one's own body highlights the camera's role as inquisitor, used by Hatoum to signify the way in which medicine confronts us with an experience of intrusion par excellence.

Discussion

What can we say about this encounter with the foreignness of images? The screen of *Foreign Body* shatters the mirror of narcissism. *Foreign Body* profoundly disturbs the relation between one's own body and the foreign body; however, this does not mean that the latter replaces the former.

From a phenomenological perspective, Jenny Slatman[3] argues that the new images of the internal body provided by medical imaging (ultrasound, endoscopy, MRI, CT and PET), affect body image as the *experienced bodily identity*. She adds: 'Because these new images – fragmented and virtually unrecognizable – are not easily integrated into the specular image of our body, we must move beyond a theory of narcissism that would reduce body image to 'visual image'.[4] Slatman therefore proposes a concept of the 'affective image.' However, it seems to me that rather than trying to use the images of the inner body to tame us, Hatoum's work shows us the anxiety of fragmentation such visual experience necessarily provokes.

What seems to be at stake here is one of the issues identified by Lacan's theory of the mirror stage. The infant recognises his specular image but cannot yet perceive that there is a difference between this image and himself: the image is 'misrecognised' (Lacan 2006: 80). The child cannot yet recognise the otherness of the image; he confuses himself with the other. The structure constructed by Mona Hatoum translates this strange alternative by imposing on us the images of the internal body, which interact with the spectator's own movements in the cabin. In the experience provided by Hatoum, the sounds and images leave us speechless; using a specular device they express a pre-specular (pre-visual) experience. Consequently, it seems to me that the culture in which we are living today is continuously offering us a wealth of images to use as mirrors in which to see ourselves reflected. It is precisely this experience of discontent that Hatoum conveys through her installation. Instead of asserting the body as one's own, the images of the internal body reveal it as strange and absent; therefore they cannot function as ideal images. No identification is possible.

The images of the internal body belong to the 'fragmented body' which precedes the imaginary unity of the mirror stage. In adult life, a regression can occur to this fragmented body, in the form of an 'aggressive disintegration of the individual,' for example in cases of hysteria or more simply in the case of a physical illness.

According to Lacan, the images of the fragmented body remain outside the visual field; they are exoscopic. They remain outside the realm of the imaginary and outside the domain of the symbolic: they are not of the order of representation. Since *Foreign Body* offers us images of the 'fragmented body,' these *endoscopic* images are in fact *exoscopic*. The figuration of the internal body cannot be integrated into body image understood as a corporeal unity. The fragmented body manifests itself at a moment when the body image is shattered. What we see here is a visual *presentation* of what cannot be *represented*, what cannot be assimilated into body image: hence its strangeness. Hatoum's *Foreign Body* can therefore be seen as a figuration of what these images of the body potentially are.

Illustrations

The medical image can be considered as an experience of the image inseparable from its enunciation. It is an image at work, an image-act, a gesture of production joined to an act of reception and contemplation. In the work of Mona Hatoum, foreignness is at the heart of her artistic message, either as an impossibility of referring oneself to a unified body, or as a message of identity disintegration which signals an impossibility of identification.

Hatoum's work deals with experiences of displacement, of disorientation, of identity reconstruction, of the disorder that generates life and of the profound feeling of discontent that stems from it.

Since World War II and the popularisation of X-ray scanning, a number of artists have used images of this kind. At first, it was to try and reflect on the inner and transparent world represented by medical imaging. This was the case for example with Francis Bacon, who in the 1950s used a radiological manual – *Positioning in Radiology*, written by Kathleen Clara Clark in 1934 – as a kind of handbook for the creation of some of his works, such as *Head Surrounded by Sides of Beef* (1954), where the artist uses X-ray images as references, in order to represent a living body in the shape of a carcass.

The diseased body is also grasped such as it is, for example in the work of another American artist, Laura Ferguson, the author of the series *The Visible Skeleton*. The artist began to experience physical deformation following an attack of acute scoliosis. At the age of 13, Ferguson underwent spine fusion surgery. The transformation of her body led her to experiment with new concepts of space and gravity, while also developing a new consciousness of certain bodily processes, such as breathing and movement. To create her pieces, Laura Ferguson initially used images from her own medical files; later she started working with files of others patients. According to the artist, the series tells the story of her own journey through illness and shows how she transformed the experience of her medicalised body into art.

Faced with the effect of the visual experience imposed on the body by these imaging techniques, the subject who is brought back to a pre-specular experience is necessarily gripped by anxiety. The artistic gesture can therefore be thought of as an act of trying to access the constituent experience of anxiety and of learning how to use it to reconstruct one's body. By incorporating and transforming the images produced by medical technology (X-rays, tomography, resonance), the artist creates a new vision of the body and redefines, among other things, the notion of the portrait, by questioning the signification of the unified image of the self.

To take another example, the Brazilian artist Monica Mansur explores the images produced by X-ray scanning, endoscopy, ultrasound and tomography, and makes them interact with cultural interpretations. Her work depicts medicalised scientific bodies in an artistic scenario. As Rosana Horio Monteiro argues in connection with Mansur's work,

> the popularization of medical images in different media contexts (cinema, television, advertising) has afforded a large public access to a perspective previously reserved to the specialized eye of a single physician. It has also contributed to the creation of a culture dependent on images and the technologies that produce them. The methods of illuminating the body's interior and its transparency have increasingly become cultural products or artifacts.[5]

In her work as a graphic designer, Monica Mansur regularly explores medical images. Since 1995, the year of her first exhibition of works produced from X-ray images and printed on adhesive tape and gauze, and until the most recent years, when she has been creating what she calls her 'crystal landscapes' or re-photographic images, Mansur explores the creative potential inherent in reproduction techniques and reflects on the esthetics of repetition.

Her re-photography works consist of re-photographed and printed images, which are based on a series of medical exams. The artist takes a photo of an image produced during an exam and then digitalises and alters it. Using this method she removes certain parts, adds or reduces the light exposure and modifies the physical space. The image is then printed on different materials, such as adhesive tape and gauze. In 1996, Mansur learned how to use video technology and created an installation with mobile images of the interior of the human stomach and colon. The images used by Mansur may be of her own body or any other: they are non-identities. Collected at random, these images can sometimes belong to the deceased, the ill and the healthy.[6]

Conclusion

What we see depends on our way of seeing. The central question of my research is the idea that considering the issues of identity raised by these specular ordeals, the main stake of clinical work with the patients who undergo them, as with any modern subject in his relationship to medicine, is to allow the subject to fabricate a gaze, a gaze which has been appropriated by the techno-scientific discourse itself.

Leroi Ghouran has shown the role technological tools play in the process of hominisation. Each historical era has its own kinds of progress, transforming the human being by making him dependent on precisely those prostheses that simultaneously open up new possibilities. This anthropological fact is confirmed by the psychoanalyst Harold Searle. In *Non-human Environment*, Searle points out that the non-human element of the human environment represents one of the most fundamental constituents of psychic life. For Searle, the ability or inability of the human being to have a constructive relationship with his non-human surroundings contributes to his psychical equilibrium or lack thereof.

Therefore, technology is far from being psychologically neutral. Faced with these body images, art invites us to free up associative thought and examine their psychological and political dimensions. It questions these dimensions with respect to identity. Psychoanalysis enables us to identify and express the psychic stakes involved in this experience. Art's way of illustrating body representation resonates in the words we hear in our everyday clinical work, in hospitals, therapy groups and other areas of the mental health system, in all the places of discussion where different perspectives meet.

Notes

1 Transference: 'Transference in psychoanalysis is essentially a displacement of emotional conduct related to an infantile object, especially the parents, onto another object or another person, especially the psychoanalyst in the course of the treatment' (Lagache 1997: 33).
2 The video is projected through a circular frame onto the floor of a cylindrical structure, which the spectator enters by one of two narrow doors situated on each side. The video footage is accompanied by a soundtrack of the sound of a heartbeat, as we can hear it from the different parts of the body examined by the camera. For about 10 minutes, the camera quickly moves along the contours of the artist's body, mostly through a back-and-forth movement, entering its various orifices.
3 Slatman (2004).
4 Ibid.
5 Horio Monteiro (2007).
6 Rosana Horio Monteiro says the following about the artist's work: 'Disindividualization of the contemporary subject is another element of the artist's work. It is the unnamed remnant of the medical examination.' 'The eye does not identify, the eye only says that this is a human body,' argues Monica Mansur. 'If this is a man or a woman, whether they are old or young, none of this can be decided without specialized medical knowledge; these medical visions exist only because they have been "imagined" through a machine, whether it is a fiber optic video camera, a magnetic wave tunnel or laser beams which produce cross-sections of organs and bones,' says Horio Monteiro, Ibid.

References

Horio Monteiro, R. (2007) 'Images médicales entre art et science.' *Sociétés*, 95(1): 97.
Slatman, J. (2004) 'L'imagerie du corps interne', *Penser le Corps*, 4. Online (no longer available).

5

PHYSICAL DISABILITY IN THE COLLECTIVE IMAGINATION

William Ebenstein

Introduction

Hephaestus is one of the 12 Olympians, a divine smith, fire-god, and gifted artisan, greatly admired for his industry and creativity. He is the only god who works and is always employed on some task of great importance for one or other of the Greek deities. In contrast to the other immortals who are distinguished by their physical beauty, Hephaestus is crippled and is considered ugly even by his own mother. The stories that are associated with Hephaestus are among the earliest writings in the Western poetic tradition related to physical disability.

A review of the historical archive reveals that he is a complex figure with many features associated with other disabled characters. His image is not limited to a single work of literature; it is ubiquitous and spans the Western imagination from the ancient Greeks to the present day. One can find early versions of some of the cultural stereotypes that are commonly associated with people with disabilities. Previously Ebenstein (2006) argued that there are differences between his portrayal in Greek literature and later representations based upon Christian, psychoanalytic and Marxist interpretations of the pagan myth.

The meaning of ancient myths may change depending on the historical context, reflecting differences in the values and practices of successive generations, but they may also resonate with their original expressions. Through a process of amplification using an array of cultural artifacts one can document creative interpretations of the Hephaestus myth. Differing versions reflect changing social attitudes and religious beliefs, shifting political and economic realities, new philosophies and psychological theories, technological advances and evolving human experiences. Although disability is a deeply felt personal experience it is also a changing social and historical phenomenon. One's individual experience of disability is embedded within this cultural tradition. Hephaestus holds an especially prominent place in the pantheon of the great personifications of disability. As a complex figure he cannot be reduced to his disability, nor can he be separated from it. Imaginative variations of the myth appear in literature, poetry, art, film, philosophy, theology, psychology and other disciplines. Creative innovations from different times and places co-exist in the collective imagination where they can be compared and contrasted with each other. In the amplification process one can study the way the Hephaestus myth has been interpreted across the ages from various ideological perspectives. The survival of a pagan god with a disability throughout the centuries provides an opportunity to chronicle the cultural history of disability. One can also continue this tradition by re-imagining the Hephaestus myth in the context of the emerging field of Disability Studies, which defines disability as a 'social construction.' It is important that Disability Studies appropriates the most iconic images of disability from the historical record. At the same time, viewing Hephaestus through a Disability Studies perspective articulates the ongoing relevance of the ancient myth within contemporary society.

A fable of rejection, resilience, resourcefulness and recovery

The classical writers are unanimous in stating that Hephaestus is thrown down from Mount Olympus. In some versions, his fall causes his limp, in others it is his disability that causes his fall. Hera is envious of the solo creation of Athene by Zeus and wants to give birth to a glorious son who can rival the bright-eyed goddess. However, Hephaestus, conceived through parthenogenesis, is born with a shrivelled foot. In shame and disgust Hera casts the infant out of Olympus so that he falls into the great sea. The rejected child is rescued by Thetis, mother of Achilles. For 9 years he remains concealed in her subterranean caverns, a secret vocational workshop, where he learns his craft. During this second incubation and apprenticeship he forges jewellery and other fine objects but also plots his return to Olympus. In other stories Hephaestus is the son of both Zeus and Hera and the situation is a marital quarrel. The young Hephaestus speaks up for his mother, and Zeus, enraged at his interference, takes him by the leg and throws him through the portals of Olympus. All day long he tumbles through space and, at sunset, falls more dead than alive on the island of Lemnos, where the barbaric-tongued Sintians find him. These versions, in which he is thrown down by either his mother or his father, and in which his disability is either congenital or caused by parental abuse, were combined throughout the centuries.

A creative mistranslation established a connection between the Greek myth, an image in the New Testament, and bitterness. According to Panofsky (1972) some scholars translated 'there he was brought up by Sintii' or 'illic nutritus ab Sintiis' as 'illic nutritus absintiis' which means 'there he was brought up on wormwood.' Wormwood is a bitter herb, the chief flavouring ingredient in absinthe. The mistranslation references the shooting star in the Book of Revelation that falls from the sky and renders the water bitter. Through the devilish connection with wormwood, Hephaestus was linked with bitterness and his limping gait became a symbol of the pollution of the soul.

Freud's writing on disability builds upon and reinforces the association with bitterness and evil. He uses Shakespeare's Richard III as the model for his analysis of personality problems of people with disabilities. Freud emphasises the bitterness with which Richard depicts his deformity to bolster the argument that virtually all people with disabilities have personality problems. Their neurotic rebelliousness is linked to their feelings of the great injustice that has been visited upon them. In Richard's case, he justifies his ruthless and immoral behavior by his grievance of being, through no fault of his own, ugly, unloved and unlovable. As noted by O'Brien (2001) many studies published in the medical and psychiatric literature reinforced Freud's conclusions by citing common personality problems of disabled people including their hostility, bitterness, and vindictiveness. Thus Freud transforms a personification of the demonic cripple into a sick one by introducing a psychiatric medical model perspective.

An alternative explanation is that in the Hephaestus case study bitterness, feelings of injustice and thoughts of revenge originate in a traumatic childhood event. However, it is not his disability but the unfair treatment at the hands of his abusive and abandoning parents that inspires the bitter outcast to re-claim his rightful place in the world. In the end his revenge is accomplished in such a clever way that it is therapeutic for the entire Olympian community.

In one story Hephaestus sends sandals as gifts to all the gods, but those he sends to his mother are made of immovable and unyielding adamantine. When she tries to walk she falls flat on her face. In this slapstick farce Hera is caught in an undignified position and publicly humiliated. At the same time Hephaestus makes fun of himself, and his own deformity. There is another famous story known as the 'binding of Hera.' In revenge for his expulsion from Olympus, Hephaestus sends a beautifully wrought golden throne to his mother as a gift. Hera sits on it with delight, but when she tries to rise again she is gripped by golden mesh fetters. The throne then rises into the air and Hera finds herself levitated as if in a magician's trick. The Olympians take council as to how they might free their queen but only Hephaestus knows the secret of the loosening. They send the divine smith a message that he should return to Olympus and set his mother free, but he replies adamantly that he has no mother. Ares, his braggart brother and sexual rival, vows to bring Hephaestus back by force, but the God of War returns to Olympus in ignominious defeat. Instead, the stubborn Hephaestus is coaxed back by Dionysius who gets him drunk. In farcical fashion the intoxicated smith is led back to Olympus atop a donkey. The carnival atmosphere of the donkey processional is part of a Dionysian shift that liberates Hephaestus from a fixation on revenge. However, the dramatic return also disrupts and transforms the social hierarchy and collective psychology of the heretofore insular Olympian community. Hephaestus is not so drunk that he would free Hera without exacting a price. He demands marriage to Aphrodite, the Goddess of Beauty.

From a Disability Studies perspective the story depicts a community that must adjust to someone who has been stigmatised, segregated, and discriminated against. The glorious fable of rejection, resilience, resourcefulness and recovery presages the striving for social justice through protest demonstrations, and the legal and legislative victories of the self-advocacy movement that have culminated in the uneasy inclusion of people with disabilities within the broader society. In Hephaestus we find a character who is motivated by his anger to confront a world that has discarded him. He stages a non-violent act of civil disobedience that completely shuts down Olympus. It is the disabled character himself who creates the humorous situation as an effective tool to confront his oppression and challenge the existing order. His stubborn anger does not lead to acceptance, adjustment or passivity. On the contrary it lifts him up to reclaim his dignity and civil rights.

The embrace of sex, violence and disability

Despite his disability and less-than-classical good looks, Hephaestus has the confidence and audacity to demand Aphrodite, the most beautiful of the goddesses, as his wife. We have a glimpse into their marital bedchamber in a scene from *The Aeneid*. Venus worries about her son Aeneas and begs her husband to forge magnificent armor for him. In the marriage bed she trades her sexual favours for weapons of war. Vulcan rises early the next morning and commands his assistants, the Cyclopes, to begin work on the armaments requested by his wife.

There is an often told story of Aphrodite's infidelity with Ares. Helios, the Sun, spies them in the act of lovemaking and informs Hephaestus who determines to catch the two in their illicit sexual activity. He hangs an invisible net over his bedposts and pretends to depart for his workshop. As soon as he leaves, Ares steals into the house and embraces Aphrodite. The net drops down upon them. Meanwhile Hephaestus retraces his steps and calls out to the other gods to witness his errant wife and her lover caught in a compromising position. Hephaestus blames her adulterous affair on his lameness. According to Edwards (2004) lameness is a characteristic associated with ugliness, an 'ungraceful unevenness,' and a 'cosmetic defect' that contrasts with the Greek ideals of physical beauty and symmetry of the body. In Greek mythology Hephaestus's limp has an aesthetic meaning. After being rejected by his mother he is now betrayed by his wife because he is hideous and deformed.

In this comic burlesque and public shaming Hephaestus plays the role of the insulted husband. Uncontrollable laughter erupts among the gods as they gaze upon the bawdy sight. For Ares it is a humiliation too while Hephaestus wins praise for his ingenuity. Hephaestus claims that his trophy wife has cheated on him because he is ugly and disabled. As in the story of the binding of Hera hurt feelings are tempered by laughter. Although his masculinity is compromised Hephaestus does not exhibit weakness or passivity and refuses the role of the violent jealous husband. In freeing the lovers he chooses a peaceful settlement but only after Poseidon guarantees to pay the 'price of adultery' on behalf of Ares.

Lowenthal (1995) studied various interpretations of the story in literature, painting, the graphic arts and sculpture. Some versions focus on tragic betrayal and wounded pride while others including many Christian commentators emphasise a moralistic message. Still others offer more practical or humorous advice. A fourteenth-century monk observed that the marriage was doomed from the start because 'when ugly husbands are mismatched with beautiful wives, adultery is sure to follow.' Janson (1952) describes a mock-heroic version of the story from the Renaissance. Vulcan, rather than Venus, is carrying on an illicit love affair. She is furious and dispatches Mercury to the island of Lemnos to stop it. Mercury finds the island populated by apes and Vulcan in love with the most beautiful simian maiden. According to Panofsky (1972) several post-classical scholars translated 'there he was brought up by Sintii' or 'illic nutritus ab Sintiis' as 'illic nutritus ab simiis' or 'there he was brought up by apes.' This playful translation provides an unexpected context that informs the reading of the myth. The association with apes reinforces the idea of parody and 'aping' that is connected with Hephaestus's comic persona. It is also a form of derision because apes were considered ugly imitations of human beings in the same way that Hephaestus was considered a deformity of the Olympian ideal of physical beauty.

In a modern context literary critics Hinz and Teunissen (1985) refer to the Ares–Aphrodite–Hephaestus Complex that pervades the D.H. Lawrence novel, *Lady Chatterley's Lover*. They see the crippled god embodied in war veteran Clifford Chatterley, the unsympathetic wheelchair-bound husband. However, in this fictional twist it is the beautiful, healthy, young wife who is victimised, frustrated both sexually and emotionally, because she is tied to an impotent invalid with a crippled soul. Trapped in a loveless marriage, she takes a lover. This theme, referred to by disabilities scholar Louis Battye (1966) as the *Chatterley Syndrome*, builds upon the idea that once a person becomes crippled he is no longer a man. In ceasing to be a sexual being Clifford is essentially defrauding his wife.

Psychoanalytic interpretations have emphasised the themes of sexual inadequacy and deviance. According to Slater (1968) this story of adultery is an 'exercise in self-humiliation' and 'self-emasculation.' Stein (1973) suggests that the failure of his marriage to Aphrodite is related to his 'Mother complex.' His crippled feet give 'an obvious clue' to 'problematic sexuality.' A psycho-sexual interpretation of the Hephaestus myth that focuses on castration or incest motifs places the blame for Aphrodite's infidelity on the disabled victim. However in the story promiscuous Aphrodite remains true to her own archetype. She is not associated with marital fidelity. Indeed, she inspired and actively aided the adultery between Paris and Helen that led to the Trojan War.

In the amplification process Chatterley can be contrasted with another wounded veteran depicted in the 1978 film *Coming Home*. The story is a love triangle between a beautiful young woman named Sally, her gung-ho Marine husband, and Luke, a disabled Vietnam vet. The film revolves around the adulterous relationship between Sally and Luke and depicts a man with disabilities as attractive and sexually active. It also turns a wounded warrior into an outspoken critic of a war that he participated in. In so doing Luke reclaims his masculine honour and sexual identity. He is transformed from a tragic victim, an angry, bitter paraplegic institutionalised in a VA hospital, into an anti-war activist, friend and lover.

In civil society an alarming increase in disabilities resulting from gun-related domestic, street and gang violence has become a public health concern. Psychologist James Hillman (2005) refers to the ready access to guns in the context of the Hephaestus myth:

> today you may pick up a fearful beauty that holds Ares, Aphrodite, and Hephaestus all together in a fine piece of metalwork at your local gun dealer. Like the steel net that entrapped the lovers, the weapon is another Hephaestian instrument holding beauty and violence in permanent embrace.... Human beings love their weapons, crafting them with the skills of Hephaestus and the beauty of Aphrodite for the purposes of Ares.
>
> *(Hillman 2005: 124–125)*

A significant segment of the American population is caught up in a frightening love affair with guns, an almost fetish-like desire to buy, collect, display and brandish firearms. In Greek mythology the most beautiful goddesses ask the armourer Hephaestus to fashion weapons either for themselves or their favourite warriors. At the same time the mythic gunsmith is known as a peacemaker who prefers to use laughter rather than weapons to settle disputes. In the story of adultery the illicit liaison between the beautiful Aphrodite and the violent Ares is put on public display and rejected by the Olympians. The comic resolution of the story is not the binding but the unbinding of Ares and Aphrodite, which forces them apart, and frees the broader community from their dangerous, forbidden embrace.

Reclaiming the historic link between disability and work

Although Hephaestus is accepted back to Olympus, it is as a second class citizen, divine servant and labourer. As the only god who works, his true home remains his workshop. He is also the most physically vivid of all the Olympians, frequently depicted as a robust smith, middle-aged, with a bearded face, a powerful thick neck and heavily muscled arms. The 'Forge of Vulcan' is a popular subject in art history with various depictions by painters such as Breugel, Rubens, Velázquez, van Dyck and others. In these personifications Hephaestus looms large and distinguished. He can be identified by his anvil and forge, wielding a hammer and tongs, working with metals, and crafting wondrous objects such as the sublime Shield of Achilles.

His poetic workshop is specifically designed to accommodate his disability. Of particular interest to the field of Disability Studies is his work in the area of assistive technology, accommodations in the workplace, and his creation of mechanical objects that function as automata. He built self-animated tripods with golden wheels that move back and forth at the gods' assemblies and which perform the work of robot servants. He also utilises voice-activated bellows. Hephaestus's powerful torso is balanced precariously on his weak legs. In order to steady his unsure steps he fashions beautiful crutches, two golden statues that resemble living girls. They hasten to his side and assist him as he walks. Thus, his crutches are transformed from emblems of weakness and dependency to ones of power and independence. These golden maidservants could not only speak and use their limbs but were also endowed with intelligence. His creations include other machines that imitate the behaviour of living beings such as Talos the giant bionic bronze man who had Olympian blood in his veins. For travels away from his volcanic workshop, Hephaestus is depicted riding in a magnificent winged wheelchair-like chariot. However, the underground forge, located in the bowels of Mother Earth, is his true home. Here he is surrounded by a crew of oddly shaped assistants including giant one-eyed Cyclopes, dwarf miners, and ancient smiths who are also personifications of tools.

In some versions of the myth, Hera gave birth to Hephaestus from her thigh in an effort to compete with Zeus' solo birthing of Athene from his head. In other versions it is Hephaestus who assists in Athene's birth by splitting Zeus' head with an axe. In either case these two deities, brother and sister have been paired from the beginning. In the Homeric Hymn they are depicted as the founders of civilisation who taught men practical arts. In this vision of *homo faber* and the rise of humanity through technology, the lame god is cast as a culture hero. Yet, Homer's Hephaestus stands in stark contrast with his portrayal by many Christian poets and scholars who made a connection between the fire-god who is thrown down from Olympus and another fallen angel. The association of Hephaestus and Lucifer is explicit in Milton's *Paradise Lost* where he is numbered among Satan's attendants.

Different images of technology emerge from different visions of the origins of civilisation. In the Homeric Hymn early human beings are depicted as living in caves like wild beasts before using fire, inventing tools, and learning practical skills. Compare this with the Christian image of the garden, an unspoiled pastoral landscape defiled by the noisy engines and polluted waters associated with technology and industrial progress. In the latter context Hephaestus's trickiness becomes a sign of a malevolent nature; his limping gait becomes a symbol of a crooked soul; the 'sweat of his brow' is a reminder of his fall from grace.

The popularity of the story of Hephaestus's return to Olympus in the sixth century B.C. marked the emergence of a new kind of city-state in Athens and a rise in the status of the city's artisans. The inclusion of the working class into the aristocracy of the Olympian order signaled a new leadership that incorporated the forces of social progress personified by culture-hero gods like Hephaestus. In the eighteenth century technological developments in Britain including iron manufacturing, improvements in machine tools, and the widespread use of coal which resulted in a new world order. Fournier D'Albe (1925) explicitly associated the advent of the Industrial Revolution with Hephaestus' return to power as the god of the Machine Age. As a noble craftsman and working class hero his 'arm and hammer' became a ubiquitous symbol for organised labour.

The technological innovations associated with industrial society led to changes in the organisation of production. Hephaestus's artisan workshop evolved into the modern factory which required a new breed of worker, subject to rationalisation and control. It required human beings to function mechanically as virtual automata.

At the same time, as noted by L. Marx (1967), many social commentators became disgusted by the ugliness, pollution and human suffering associated with the new factory system. Rather than being connected with progress and the rise of civilisation as portrayed in the Homeric Hymn, industrialisation and machine technology were viewed by some as the evil antithesis of the quiet pastoral garden. This narrative of the Hephaestus myth incorporates the exploitation of the working class, and hellish working conditions resulting in disabilities caused by industrial accidents. Unlike craft workers, industrial workers were subject to the conformity of the assembly line and their bodies became interchangeable parts of a machine. Employment policies excluded people with disabilities from working in standardised environments designed for the average worker. This widespread practice was endorsed even by labour unions that were focused on securing disability benefits for workers who were injured on the job rather than integrating injured workers and other people with disabilities into the workplace.

The lesson of the ancient myth is that people with disabilities can thrive and excel in the workplace. Hephaestus's workshop served as an icon for the Athenian craft guilds. Even today the incorporation of this vision into actual work environments could enhance opportunities for quality jobs and meaningful employment for people with and without disabilities. His shop provides a mythic model for a futuristic workplace that applies universal design elements, and incorporates technology and individualised accommodations to tap the productive energies of all workers. Here the creative soul of the worker is valued and technology and artistic design are used to accommodate individual differences.

Conclusion

An essential aspect of the Disability Studies philosophy is its definition of disability as a 'social construction.' The social construction of the disabled body has deep roots in the collective imagination, and Hephaestus plays a prominent role in this history. The Disability Studies discipline can appropriate this tradition by re-interpreting the myth through its more contemporary perspective. Through the centuries, the Greek ideal that equated symmetry of the body with beauty, the Christian tradition that often linked a limping gait with a crooked soul, the psychoanalytic approach that transformed a demonic cripple into a sick one, have dominated the discourse, reinforced each other, and created a construct that defined the disabled body as ugly, evil and ill. Disability Studies can offer a counter-narrative, one that looks at the very same stories and finds new meanings.

The Hephaestus myth is part of a long tradition in Western literature of using disability for comic purposes. His practical jokes give rise to 'inextinguishable laughter,' among his fellow Olympians. Brown (1998) identifies Hephaestus as a 'trickster.' In spite of the 'friendly-cruel' laughter that may be directed at him he remains a powerful and magical figure. It is he who conceives and executes clever pranks to achieve a specific purpose. His genius is based upon an ability to mimic others, but also to parody his own disability. He is able to embarrass others because he is willing to be embarrassed himself. Since anyone may be a target of mockery, Hephaestus, the disabled trickster, creates a comedy of equality in which everyone in the Olympian leisure class has an equal right to be ridiculed and humiliated. Through the comic genre Hephaestus' conflicts with his mother, brother and wife are resolved in a peaceful manner.

For literary critic and Disability Studies scholar Leonard Kriegel, Hephaestus represents a living inspiration that resonates with his own experience of disability. In his essay, *Bodily Passions: Hephaestus among the Gods*, he describes his profound identification with the mythic character.

> And so I watch the lame god push his body through the heavens of Olympus, and my own cripple's heart fills with envy of and admiration for this brother in the kingdom of the crippled, my shining example of the will to endure.
>
> *(Kriegel 1998: 76)*

Hephaestus's 'will to endure' despite his physical limitations reminds Kriegel of his own grudging anger and resentment and sees in the disabled deity a defiant hero. Hephaestus is an example of what Kriegel terms a 'survivor cripple,' a tough-minded, courageous hero, at once disabled and enabled, an active conscious agent who refuses to play the role of the victim or outcast and is able to impose his presence on the world.

Through a Disability Studies interpretation of the ancient myth, the crippled god may be viewed as an icon of a strength-based approach to physical disability. He displays courage, confidence and practical intelligence along with humility and good humour. Part of his independence derives from his assistive technology which includes a winged wheelchair, voice activated machinery, intelligent robots and other clever devices that support him in navigating the physical environment, the world of work and the social hierarchy. By critically reviewing the evolution of socially constructed representations of disability such as Hephaestus, Disability Studies can open up a broader discussion of the place of disability in our own popular culture.

References

Battye, L. (1966) 'The Chatterly syndrome', in P. Hunt (ed.), *Stigma: The Experience of Disability*. London: Geoffrey Chapman.

Brown, M.L. (1998) 'Hephaestus, Hermes, and Prometheus: Jesters to the Gods', in V. Janik (ed.), *Fools and Jesters in Literature, Art and History*. Westport: Greenwood Press.

Ebenstein, W. (2006) 'Toward an archetypal psychology of disability based on the Hephaestus myth', *Disability Studies Quarterly*. Online. Available HTTP: <http://dsq-sds.org/issue/view/37>. Accessed: 7 November, 2013.

Edwards, M.L. (2004) 'Constructions of physical disability in the ancient Greek world: The community concept', in D.T. Mitchell and S.L. Snyder (eds), *The Body and Physical Difference: Discourses of Disability*. Ann Arbor: The University of Michigan Press.

Fournier D'Albe, E.E. (1925) *Hephaestus or The Soul of the Machine*. New York: E.P. Dutton.

Freud, S. (1958) 'Some character-types met with in psycho-analytic work', in B. Nelson (ed.) *On Creativity and the Unconscious*. New York: Harper and Row.

Graves, R. (1974) *The Greek Myths*. Baltimore: Penguin Books.

Hillman, J. (2005) *A Terrible Love of War*. New York: Penguin Books.

Hinz, E.J. and Teunissen, J.J. (1985) 'War, love and industrialism: The Ares/Aphrodite/Hephaestus complex in Lady Chatterley's Lover', in M. Squires and D. Jackson (eds), *D.H. Lawrence's 'Lady': A New Look at Lady Chatterley's Lover*. Athens: University of Georgia Press.

Homer (1971) *The Illiad*. Translated by Lattimore, R. Chicago: University of Chicago.

Homer (1968) *The Odyssey* Translated by Lattimore, R. New York: Harper and Row.

Janson, H.W. (1952) *Apes and Ape Lore in the Middle Ages and Renaissance*. London: Warburg Institute.

Kerenyi, C. (1974) *The Gods of the Greeks*. London: Thames and Hudson.

Kriegel, L. (1987) 'The cripple in literature', in A. Gartner and T. Joe (eds) *Images of the Disabled, Disabling Images*. New York: Praeger.

Kriegel, L. (1998) 'Bodily passions: Hephaestus among the Gods', in *Flying Solo*. Boston: Beacon Press.

Longmore, P.K. (1987) 'Screening stereotypes: Images of disabled people in television and motion pictures', in A. Gartner and T. Joe (eds) *Images of the Disabled, Disabling Images*. New York: Praeger.

Lowenthal, A.E. (1995) *Joachim Wtewael: Mars and Venus Surprised by Vulcan*. Malibu: The J. Paul Getty Museum.

Marx, L. (1967) *The Machine in the Garden: Technology and the Pastoral Ideal in America*. New York: Oxford University Press.

Milton, J. (1962) *Paradise Lost*. New York: Holt, Rinehart and Winston.

Mitchell, D.T. and Snyder, S.L. (2001) 'Representations and its discontents: The uneasy home of disability in literature and film', in G.L. Albrecht, K.D. Seelman and M. Bury (eds) *Handbook of Disability Studies*. Thousand Oaks: Sage Publications.

O' Brien, R. (2001) *Crippled Justice*. Chicago: University of Chicago Press.

O'Brien, R. (2005) *Bodies in Revolt: Gender, Disability, and a Workplace Ethic of Care*. New York: Routledge.

Panofsky, E. (1972) *Studies in Iconology*. New York: Harper and Row.

Rose, M.L. (2006) *The Staff of Oedipus: Transforming Disability in Ancient Greece*. Ann Arbor: University of Michigan Press.

Sargent, T. (1973) *The Homeric Hymns: A Verse Translation*. New York: W.W. Norton & Co.

Slater, P.E. (1968) *The Glory of Hera*. Princeton: Princeton University Press.

Stein, M. (1973) 'Hephaistos: A pattern of introversion', in J. Hillman (ed.) *Spring*. New York: Spring Publications.

Stiker, H. (2002) *A History of Disability*. Translated by W. Sayers. Ann Arbor: University of Michigan Press.

Virgil (1951) *The Aeneid*. Translated by R. Humphries. New York: Charles Scribner's Sons.

6

THE DISABLED BODY IN CONTEMPORARY SOCIETY

Simone Korff Sausse

Introduction

Identity construction is a dynamic process which combines individual and cultural factors. Identity changes constantly with age and life events. It involves the body as we start from the hypothesis that body image is one of the constitutive elements of identity. The purpose of this chapter is to reflect on the interactions between contemporary identity and body image, in the special case when the body is disabled. And what about the identity of a disabled person in contemporary society?

Disability is a cultural fact that calls up processes that are at once individual and universal. To what extent are the psychic effects brought out by the disability determined by socio-cultural variables, and thus different depending on historical period or cultural area, and to what extent are they psychic processes observable in a universal way in spite of – or over and above – various factors imprinted by cultural and social data (Stiker 1982)? Referring to elements borrowed from mythology, anthropology, history, literature and art allows us to enrich our understanding and to point out ideological presuppositions.

A psychoanalyatic approach allows us better to understand the unconscious individual and collective representations brought up by disability, that produce an impression of 'the uncanny' and which are the origin of stigmatisation and exclusion (Goffman 1963). The body image linked to disability, as it appears in the clinical situations psychoanalysts deal with, gives us some cues to better understand the contemporary characteristics of identity, even when not concerned with disability.

We can postulate that the anthropological mutations of our society, which affect the image of the body and identity, reshape the collective unconscious representations created by disability. New technologies, which considerably improve the life of certain disabled people, have an impact on the image of the body in general. These new technologies are likely to modify the status of the disabled person, which is akin to that of the contemporary body. The treatment of the body in contemporary art, bodily transformations, hybrid bodies, cyborgs, etc. generalise the impression of the 'uncanny', which does not characterise only disabled persons. Furthermore, recent contributions by neuroscience (concerning the plasticity of the brain, mirror neurons, implicit memory, etc.) modify the conception of disability and identity. It is very interesting to see that gender studies and disability studies raise the same questions about our habitual categories. Disability studies are very similar to gender studies, as both lead us to re-examine not only the difference between the masculine and the feminine, but also the difference between disabled and able-bodied. The situation of the disabled subject strangely resembles 'other kinds', for the disabled person, like the intersexes, finds him/herself in an in-between situation, with an indeterminate status. This status links up with the idea of inter-breeding, which I consider as a paradigm of the contemporary identity.

Clinical background and psychoanalysis

The clinical background of this work is the practice from a psychoanalytical point of view with disabled children and their family. For many years, specialists did not pay much attention to people with disabilities in general, and to the child with disabilities in particular. One spoke about the child; it was never the turn of the child to speak. The object of study, analysis and commentary, he or she was not imagined as having knowledge about him or herself. In fact, the situation was never imagined from the point of view of the child. It is the same with adults with intellectual disability or those who have some kind of disability due to illness or an accident or ageing.

The psychoanalyst has an ethical position, which depends on a double conviction. First of all, every human being, no matter what their condition, has something to say about his or her subjective position, his situation in the world, his 'Weltanschauung'. And secondly, the psychoanalyst has something to listen to. Indeed, in spite of mental impairment, leading to a psychic apparatus presenting limits in capacity to elaborate events, persons with a disability, even those who are very lacking in intellectual terms, make themselves interpreters of their difference; interpreters of their becoming; interpreters of their strangeness, of their estrangement. The infirmity arrives and violently stirs up questions of origin and causality. It becomes necessary at all costs to find an explanation for this abnormality (Canguilhem 1943), launching forth on a quest of causality where beliefs, superstitions and magic are mixed.

The principal representations brought up by disability have three axes:

- Faulty filiation: the abnormality is experienced as punishment for an incestuous fault that it unveils and reveals.
- Dangerous transmission: the abnormality comes to show in a painful and anxiety-provoking way that we do not master the process of transmission, as

we would like to believe, and as the scientific illusion would like to make us believe. We do not know what we transmit; we do not know what has been transmitted to us.
- Forbidden procreation. It follows that one must stop filiation and transmission; one must stop procreation.

These are the representations that are activated by disability and that weigh heavy on the life experience of the person with disabilities who is constantly confronted with them, in the look of the others (Winnicott 1974).

Disability and trauma

Whatever the reason, the disability of the body is a traumatic event, presenting all the characteristics described by Freud and Ferenczi. Trauma holds in check the ability of the ego to assimilate emotions and incites a psychic state we can link to fright. We know that Freud differentiated between fright, fear and anxiety. Fright is the state which occurs when one faces a dangerous situation unprepared, it accentuates the surprise factor. Ferenczi develops at length this aspect of trauma in terms of fragmentation, atomisation and partial destruction of the mind following a trauma. 'An unexpected, unprepared for, overwhelming shock acts, as if it were, [as] an anaesthetic. How can this be? Apparently by inhibiting every kind of mental activity and thereby provoking a state of complete passivity devoid of any resistance' (Ferenczi [1931]1955: 239). The shock of discovering the disability has a destructive effect on the psyche. This in turn creates an open wound in the psyche itself which unceasingly and vainly tries to close. The customary mechanisms of defense are held in check and pathological mechanisms may appear. 'Nothing is the same any more', say the parents of a disabled child, much as might persons who have been through traumatic experiences like war or tsunami, or who have had a stroke or an accident causing a disability of the body and/or the mind.

But Ferenczi also considers that these mechanisms are survival strategies. I wonder actually if the trauma and the accompanying inability to think could not be considered as a way of short-circuiting an unbearable link. It would have, therefore, a double function of blocking the thinking process, but also of protecting the survival of psychic life, similar to hibernation. One can refer here to the theory of Bion (1963, 1970) who postulates that at the beginning of psychic life (which he places before birth, during the intra-uterine period), there is an emotional experience which looks for a way to be represented. 'Thoughts searching for an apparatus to think them'. The psyche develops the capacity to think these corporal and emotional experiences in an intersubjective relation. Parents will be confronted by this situation: an unthinkable thought occurs to them and, according to Bion's terminology, the subject is led to create an apparatus which allows him/her to think 'thoughts which have already emerged'. The work of the psychoanalyst will be to promote this linking process and bring expression to where there was only silent pain.

Freud's last theory of trauma (1938) attributes to trauma a negative and positive function. He was in fact inspired, without mentioning it, by the ideas of Ferenczi and postulated that if analysis could bring the patient to relive the unsettling trauma, 'a new sort of resolution of the trauma, more positive, more long term, could take place'. A repetition of the trauma could, therefore, promote a more favorable integration into psychic life of what would otherwise remain split off like 'a State within a State' and as such would become, according to Freud, 'an inaccessible party with which cooperation is impossible' (1938: 76).

Contemporary body and disabled body

The notion of disability can be extended to many different situations which I put together under the notion of 'extreme bodies', including a certain number of bodily situations (disabled body, body of the extremely premature baby, injured body, reanimated body, body of a badly burnt person, body of an elderly person, transsexual body, body in the terminal stage of illness, etc.), all of which have the common feature of leading us to the frontiers of the human.

In these cases, the person is faced with a change of appearance and bodily suffering that is imposed on him by life (illness, handicap or accident), of which he is in a way the victim. He will have to deal with it actively and eventually try to repair. Here we are in the realm of trauma theory. But in other cases, the person himself seeks this change of appearance. He is the agent of it. In this sense, he challenges and transgresses the biological facts of bodily reality. This is what characterises the contemporary body image. Are we faced in modernity with a human being reduced technically to his organs? A body that is a fabricated product? Can it be said that the subjection of human beings to the steamroller of a reductive ideology (subjecting them to evaluative control and the ideal of performance) means that there is no longer either a subject in culture or a patient in clinical practice? However, we can have a more optimistic point of view, when we seek fruitful analogies between:

- on the one hand the clinical issues that are mobilised in the somatic affections of the body in patients.
- and, on the other, the approaches of contemporary artists who give a major place to the body in their works or performances and who, in spite of the apparent dehumanisation, manage to achieve real creations.

It is indeed surprising to observe that there are many similarities between the disabled body and the contemporary body, especially as it appears in artistic realisations.

In the case of imposed disability, due to birth, illness, accident or ageing, we can observe contrasting movements of de-symbolisation and symbolisation. Extreme bodies are at once the object of symbolic deconstruction and dehumanisation, but are also the locus of unexpected and unusual symbolisations which permit the subject to be re-humanised.

Clinically, I have seen this in my encounter with severely disabled children. These children live with a damaged and weak body, one that has been so manipulated by surgical operations, and fitted out with prostheses, that it appears non-human. But astonishingly, their bodily and identificatory image is intact at the level of symbolisation, subjectivity, and thus of humanity.

In the case of accidental disability, the body, which seems to be self-evident, which is felt to have unity and continuity, and is a source of natural and unquestioned sensations, becomes a stranger the patient will have to live with. When the body is healthy, there is a state of concordance between the self-image as it appears in the mirror or in the other's eyes and the self-image that the subject has within himself. In the case of an accident, mutilation, disfiguring, this concordance becomes discordance.

It now becomes a figure of uncanniness, a persecutor, an enemy. The disability constitutes an event which embodies something unthinkable and horrifying, and therefore calls to mind the idea of the uncanny ('Unheimliche') described by Freud (1919). Among the figures of the uncanny Freud presents that of illness linked to the idea of deficiency: 'The uncanny effect of epilepsy or madness has the same origin. The layman sees in them the working of forces hitherto unsuspected in his fellow-men, but at the same time, he is dimly aware of them in remote corners of his own being'.

The tetraplegic poet Joë Bousquet (Bousquet 1941) is an example of the absolute gap when a human being, owing to neurological illness or serious motor infirmity, finds himself imprisoned in his body, deprived of all the means necessary for expressing himself. In 1918, at the age of 21, Bousquet received a bullet in the spinal cord during the battle of Vailly, which left him tetraplegic. Until his death in 1950, he spent his existence immobilised on a bed that he would never leave, in a room with closed shutters. There, he was visited by artists and poets, men and women, with whom he established intense relationships. He produced texts continually (diaries, novels, poems, love letters and an erotic novel). He gives others the impression that he has an uninhabited body, that there is of an absence of subject, whereas in fact there is an internal world of thoughts, fantasies, affects and images, that is, a subjective presence, but one that he can neither formulate nor share. As Bousquet puts it, it is an 'absurd body' to which he is bound by intolerable yet indissoluble ties. 'I felt like a mind harnessed to a corpse.' The disabled body causes a split and becomes a persecutor. This body doesn't belong to him. He is dispossessed of it. The body is manipulated, treated, spoken by the others.

Who is the subject of this desubjectivised body? This body is marked by the stamp of alterity; and one may wonder if this alterity is not irreducible, leading to the fringes of humanity, the inhuman, especially when, with the new technologies, this body is fitted out with prostheses or equipped with implants. Moreover, the others, and sometimes the care-givers, have difficulty in not being captivated by the fascinating and alienating specular aspects of the extreme body. It brings the infirm or deformed person back to this painful split between an internal humanity and an external inhumanity.

Creation or symptom?

In the second situation, a person deliberately inflicts harm on his body. These clinical situations cover a very wide spectrum ranging from ordinary aesthetic operations to radical and mutilating bodily transformations. The aim is to modify an aspect of the external appearance, which is felt to be unsightly or not in line with the self-image, and to make it coincide with this internal image. Anyway, they consist in changing their body image in order to change their identity. How are such acts to be understood? As creation or symptom? Are they to be seen as part of a psychopathological organisation or do they belong to an aesthetic, or even philosophical and existential process?

David Le Breton (2006), a French sociologist working in the field of historical anthropology of the body, says that scarification should not be considered as pathology, but as a strategy of survival, a remedy, a way of giving form to sufferings. It's a way of re-appropriating the body. Paradoxically, pain gives a sense of existence again to a body that is on the verge of collapse.

Unless, that is, the aim is precisely to establish a concordance between the appearance of the body and a damaged, even monstrous, internal image. But there is discordance, too, when a person of apparently 'normal' physical appearance undergoes practices of transformation, or even mutilation (operations, tattooing, piercing), in order to modify a healthy body into an altered body, a body that deviates from the human model.

Curiously enough, the subject recognises himself in this new transformed and damaged body. He doesn't recognise himself in the body that was given to him, and he often says that he has never recognised himself in it. He constructs a new body for himself which corresponds to the internal image and to his identity. The most spectacular and radical example of this process is that of those who have chosen to have amputations: 'for the first time in my life I had the impression that my body was complete, that it's my body and that it corresponds to my identity', said one person.

With these persons (can one use the word patients?) the aim is to make the body's appearance conform to the internal image. The body subjected to transformations is a projected surface of destructive, split and mutilated internal objects.

In these situations, we are caught up in a dialectic of the visible and invisible, of appearance and interiority, of the human and inhuman. One can be beautiful on the inside and ugly on the outside, just like the little duckling and the wonderful swan. One can be animal externally and human internally (*Beauty and the Beast*; Kafka's *Metamorphosis*). One can be human on the outside and animal on the inside (the great tyrant-monsters of twentieth-century political history).

In these desires for bodily transformations one can identify identificatory images with waste, with the animal, with the bestial pregenital level, with the monster. In the case of these adolescents, as with some artists, the issue is one of making the outside concur with the inside. Inner dirt, abject waste, has to be objectified on the visible surface of the body.

In the domain of extreme clinical situations, one always meets with the category of animality. People suffering from a disability, an abnormality of development, a deformity, mental deficiency, the terminal phases of illness, extreme prematurity, old age, inevitably evoke images of bestiality, in the sense of an overflow of impulses indicating that the anthropological barrier that guarantees the difference between human and animal has been crossed.

An interesting parallel can be drawn here with the approaches of many contemporary artists who have recourse to animality. Animality makes it possible to explore alternative and experimental worlds, to go beyond frontiers, whether they be aesthetic or anthropological, and to denounce the false humanistic ideologies of society. The issue is to overcome the binary opposition man/animal and to experiment with other organisations of identity.

William Wegman makes his dog, called Man Ray in tribute to the Surrealist photographer, one of the main subjects of his work. But other artists go still further: Oleg Koulik, for instance, during a performance, exhibits himself naked, on all fours, imitating a nasty dog. For him, 'it is a way of showing the disarray of the painter who can't express himself any more with canvases and brushes, who gets down on all fours and is reduced to his animal instincts.' It is a metaphor used by the artist to expose the animal nature of human beings. Oleg Koulik adds that it was in the army that he discovered the animality of human beings.

These artists reveal the dimension of animality in us – the limits of the human. But paradoxically, animality allows us to think something about the human realm, which would not otherwise be thinkable. What is difficult to think about is not the animal, but that which is human. The animal is a mirror that allows us to question the identity and nature of the human. This is evidenced by the figure of the animal in certain remarkable works of art: Goya's dog, Miro's dog, Franz Marc's horses ('do horses dream?' this painter wondered), and then Giacometti's emaciated and scraggy dog which may be considered as a tragic self-portrait.

The body image: from Christian iconography to modern art

The tendency in artistic creation to give prominence to the ugliness and suffering of the human body – a marked tendency of contemporary art – has its roots in Christian iconography. From the end of the Middle Ages onwards, we can observe the development, in painting and sculpture, of extreme bodies with the expansion of the theme of Christ's Passion, starting with Grünewald's determining work, the Issenheim Altarpiece, in Colmar.

Saints and martyrs flagellated, stigmatised, dislocated, burnt, cut up, skinned alive, bleeding, disembowelled, enucleated (evoking scarified bodies), are evocative of the scarified, tattooed, cannibalised and faecalised bodies depicted by modern artists. Job, on his pile of dung, covered from top to bottom by a malignant ulcer, is nothing but a stinking and repulsive body, as presented to the spectator by the Viennese action artists. Saint Sebastian's body riddled with arrows, exhibited in galleries for centuries, has been used intensely in contemporary art, in particular by gay artists, as an icon of homosexuality.

This tradition attests to the fact that Western art is deeply rooted in the context of Christianity, even if many contemporary artists prefer to forget or deny these roots. The development of painting emerged from the debate between iconophiles and iconoclasts. What made it possible to overcome the iconoclasts' prohibition on representation was the theological principle of the incarnation, that is, of the double nature of Christ.

For Paul Klee, the aim of painting was to 'make the invisible visible'. In saying this, Klee was perhaps not aware that this claim had its source in debates on the invisibility of the divine and the possibility or prohibition of representing it, which, following the iconophiles and iconoclasts, continued across the centuries. The issue here is that a man is made in the image of God, whose representation will make visible, in its human form, the invisible divine nature. Christ is the visible aspect of the Father, and the Father the invisible aspect of Christ. If Christ has a double nature, human and divine, every human being participates in his turn in divine nature.

It is the humanisation of Christ, based on the principle of the incarnation, which makes the representation of ugliness possible. In other words, ugliness is there to evoke Christ's human character. Another important point is that ugliness is associated with the idea of suffering, which can be seen in contemporary art and particularly in body art. With the principle of incarnation, suffering is the lot both of the divine being and of humans. Ugliness is no longer that which comes and disturbs the order of the world and the ideal of Beauty, as in Antiquity, but depicts on the contrary that which is specifically human. Furthermore, this ugly character becomes a figure of identification, for he is representative of the human condition, something which is brought into play in body performances and actions. Is this not a way of playing with the limits of humanity, one that aims apparently at eliminating the human element, while also contributing to its demonstration?

Conclusion

Imposed bodily modifications and chosen bodily modifications have common points. Indeed clinical practice shows us that the trauma (in these cases: illness, disability) can never be reduced to destiny, for it produces psychic processes aimed at elaborating this destiny. Even if the reason for the abnormality of the body is fortuitous, due to chance or to the unforeseeable and uncontrollable nature of somatic life, the person feels the need to realise a subjective appropriation of this traumatic event, which sometimes involves resorting to perverse mechanisms in order to master a reality that is imposed and ineluctable. Thus one sees disabled children employing perverse strategies, such as provocation and exhibitionism, to deal with the unthinkably arbitrary nature of the handicap. An illustration of this position can be found in the painter Toulouse-Lautrec and the writer Mishima (Korff-Sausse [2000] 2010), as well as in the work of Frida Kahlo. The person who mutilates himself is perhaps striving for a paradoxical form of reparation.

The disabled person holds out a mirror unmasking our own proper imperfections, reflecting an image of ourselves we have no desire to see. This person has been stamped as strange. From being strange, he may become a persecutor, for he exposes our own strangeness. 'He played a dirty trick on us', said the father of a child who has Down's syndrome. According to Freud, that which appears strange in reality is familiar. 'For what is uncanny is in reality nothing new or alien but something which is known of old and long familiar and which has become alienated from it only through the process of repression.' Is this strange person the expression of an ancient repressed figure? In other cultures, ancestors are believed to be reincarnated when a child is born, above all when the child is marked by some different characteristics. The body image in contemporary society reproduces this kind of strangeness, making strangeness linked to disability less strange. Abled or disabled are not any more opposite categories, but aspects among a multitude of others, leading to the idea of inter-breeding which can be considered as a paradigm of the contemporary identity.

References

Bion, W.R. ([1970] 1984) *Attention and Interpretation*, London: Maresfield Reprints.

Bion, W.R. ([1963] 1984) *Elements of Psycho-analysis*, London: Karnac Books.

Bousquet, J. ([1941] 1968) *Traduit du Silence*. Paris: L'imaginaire, Gallimard.

Canguilhem, G. ([1943] 1991) *Le Normal et le Pathologique*, Paris: PUF, Collection Quadrige.

Ferenczi, S. ([1931] 1955) *Final Contributions to the Problems and Methods of Psycho-analysis*, New York: Basic Books.

Freud, S. (1919) *The 'Uncanny'*, Standard Edition vol. XVII, London: Penguin, pp. 217–256.

Freud, S. (1938) *Moses and Monotheism*, Standard Edition vol. XXIII, London: Penguin, pp. 1–137.

Goffman, E. (1963) *Stigma*, London: Prentice Hall.

Korff-Sausse, S. (1996) *Le Miroir Brisé : L'Enfant Handicapé, Sa Famille et le Psychanalyste*, Paris: Calmann-Lévy.

Korff-Sausse, S. ([2000] 2010) *Figures du Handicap. Mythes, Arts, Littérature*, Paris: Petite Bibliothèque Payot.

Le Breton, D. (2006) 'Les marques du corps', *Revue Enfances & Psy*, 32.

Stiker, H.J. (2005) *Corps Infirmes et Sociétés* (1982), 3rd edition. Paris: Dunod.

Winnicott, D.W. (1974) *The Mirror Role of the Mother and Family in Child Development. Playing And Reality*. London: Routledge, pp. 11–119.

7

BODY IMAGE AND IDENTITY IN VICTIMS OF EXTREME VIOLENCE

Régine Waintrater

An extreme experience is always one that is aimed at the body – for that is the real end-point, both for the torturer and for the victim.

I mean by the term 'extreme experience' a situation such as torture or persecution in which things are pushed to their very limits, where the pact of civilisation no longer holds with respect to the life of the individual and where human beings stop being human, in their own eyes as well as in those of others. I shall try to show how extreme experiences require victims to undertake some degree of work in and on their mind and to employ language in a new way, one that affects their whole identity, transforming it in such a way as to make all modification irreversible. Because of the powerful constraints that it inflicts on the body, persecution entails a de-metaphorisation of language, which thereupon loses all notion of choice and of play; it is divested of everything, so that body and mind come together in such a manner that they can no longer be separated. One must not, all the same, draw the conclusion that those who speak that language and share it with their companions in misfortune have abandoned their identity as human beings. Nor should that language be confused with the neo-language of the torturers, because it is in fact quite the opposite of this. Torturers take possession of language in order to modify all of its words and bend them in such a way as to make them correspond to the neo-language of which they see themselves the masters, while the language of their victims, although they might have to adopt certain words as used by their torturers, cannot be reduced simply to that. Indeed, in one specific and highly important respect, it is quite different from it: the language of the torturers constantly attempts to hide the actions that it designates, by making considerable use of euphemisms. This was remarkably demonstrated by the German Jewish philologist, Victor Klemperer (1975), in his book *The Language of the Third Reich.*

Victims, on the other hand, try as best they can to find the exact words to describe what they are going through, in a movement which, beginning with the initial de-metaphorisation, follows in the reverse direction the trajectory of the individual and the species in order to be in contact once again with the texture of primary inscriptions – those that precede words, that precede indeed any feeling of unity and cohesion of the self. This attempt at re-metaphorisation is a movement that re-cathexes and focuses on the body, that inescapable end-point of the Real dimension, the source and final frontier that the mind comes up against.

The *corpus* of this section is based not only on oral and written testimonies of victims of the principal genocides of the twentieth century but also on extracts from what has come to be known as the 'literature of the camps' – by Armenians, by authors such as Améry, Antelme or Levi, and of course by prisoners of the Gulag, in particular Varlam Shalamov in his book, *The Kolyma Tales*. I have two hypotheses in mind:

1 Every extreme experience invalidates and reverses the distinction between body and mind. It draws the individual back to a time in which the mind was still corporised and the body not yet mentalised. As I have shown before in some of my previous work, the body becomes both *the object that saves* and *the object that has to be saved*, the object that is the ultimate base and support of one's sense of self (Waintrater 2003, 2010).
2 The body is the link between the present and the actual occurrence of the trauma, the mainspring of a deferred retroactive processing. In order to express the extreme experience, there is a form of writing that follows the paths of re-metaphorisation in a new direction; these new pathways will forever be superimposed on the former codes of language, thereby constituting a significant modulation of that particular culture.

How, then, does the body reverse the distinction between body and mind?

The reason is that, while the extreme experience is on-going and also once it is over, it is produced, 'secreted', by perception and sensoriality in each of its dimensions. Experienced in the body, it will shape the awareness and the memory of the events that occur – and, in so doing, it will shape the individual's identity during and after those events. The visual, tactile or sound image is generated by the body, emitted and immediately received by the affected body: it is that body which becomes both a *body-as-source*, bearing witness to the reality of persecution, and a *body-as-target*, which is being subjected to torture. According to Luba Jurgenson (2003), 'the spirit simply follows', since it is 'the body that is calling the tune'. That is why, she adds, 'a true testimony of the reality of a camp can be given only by the body'. It is the body that shows the full extent of the passage of time and space, thereby modifying the individual's hitherto familiar points of reference.

According to Freud (1914), this reversion back onto the body can be seen in all kinds of extreme situations, illness and persecution. The narcissistic libido is redistributed such that there is no distinction between it and the ego-drives. 'Here libido and ego-interest share the same fate and are once more indistinguishable from each other' (1914: 82). The reservoir (the ego) behaves like a source (the erotogenic zones), and all cathexes come from it.

Tertiary narcissism, as defined by Judith Kestemberg and Ida Brenner (1986), is derived both from primary narcissism and from secondary narcissism. It represents a return to a state that precedes ego formation, a primary state of life, autoerotic. Like primary narcissism, it has to do with cathecting the body, both as a whole and in some of its parts, which become the equivalent of parts of the mental apparatus. Like secondary narcissism, which brings about a withdrawal of the libido towards the ego, it withdraws libido from the loved external object (father, mother) and directs it towards a vital organ. Although tertiary narcissism strongly resembles primary narcissism, it is different from it insofar as it is not an-objectal – quite the contrary, in fact. It is an ultimate attempt to preserve a state of objectality, taking as its object the body and its functions.

It is, in a way, Socrates feeling with delight his blood flowing in his legs. It is Robert Antelme writing in *The Human Race*:

> Just by running his hand over his legs he would rediscover that property, shared with those at home, of having a body that belonged to him, a body he could dispose of, thanks to which he could be something complete.
>
> (1947: 27)

In the camp, the person called the *Muselmann*, as described by Primo Levi, was precisely the one person who could no longer preserve his objectality – he gave up any idea of treating his body as his ultimate object.

In times of persecution, the body is the object that must be saved – and also the object that saves. This is what I have called the significant object of survival (Waintrater 2003), which holds in its possession and guarantees the on-going continuity of one's self-identity and sense of self. Here, physical and mental survival are one and the same, through this cathexis of the body or of one of its parts. These significant objects are the transitional objects of extreme situations; they enable us to attain the oceanic feeling and to re-establish a kind of omnipotence when we are in the grip of extreme helplessness.

That is where we see the paradox of these borderline situations: it is at the point where the victim's body is completely powerless, when the aim is to dispossess the victim of his or her body, that it becomes the ultimate bastion. This has nothing to do with asceticism, as Agamben would have us believe in his drift towards aesthetics, but a return to what is fundamental. The movement is from personal attachment to *one's own life* towards an impersonal attachment to *life itself*. To paraphrase Maurice Blanchot, we could describe this as the relationship to the unadorned life of the human being reduced to the avidity of need, with no pleasure, like an egoism without an ego.

The entire sacred dimension then corresponds to life itself; that is the title that I gave to my comments on the deportation diary of a young Armenian.

A new relationship with language

The body of the concentration camp prisoner becomes a manuscript upon which we see wrinkles, the colour of cold, the toothless mouth, malnutrition, illness, approaching death. A body that speaks, that shows, that expresses without any possibility of avoidance, as in the 'selection process' in which the state of the individual's buttocks determined whether or not he or she would be sent to the gas chamber.

The marked body of the slave, the tattooed body of the prisoner in a concentration camp, the gashed body of the Tutsi, the tortured body – it is always the body that bears witness to the time in question. For anyone who attempts to convey his or her experience, language is, as it were, twofold. Each word comes to have a double layer: that of its ordinary meaning, and that of the word experienced in and through the body – thirst, hunger, cold are just a few examples.

As Charlotte Delbo puts it, this doubling of language, between 'light' words and those weighted down by the experience of the body, will never really come to an end. It is a necessary phenomenon, because otherwise someone who had felt thirsty could no longer say: 'I'm thirsty, let's have a cup of tea'. Weighted-down words create a vocabulary of economics, of intensity, built upon the narrowing of the gap between language and the body that is turned into a written document.

This was what Shalamov (1994) showed us, in his short story entitled *The Lawyers' Plot*. Before being executed, and after spending a freezing night in solitary confinement, the zeks (prisoners of the Gulag) suddenly feel a sense of wellbeing, because the surrounding air has become warmer. How do they express this? 'Through a sudden urge to urinate.' 'By what other way could we tell the soldiers that we were glad of the warmth and of the southern wind?'

Or *The Human Race*, which begins: 'I went outside to take a piss'. The words of the body have recovered their original meaning and strength, in a poetical form of economy that simultaneously impoverishes and enriches them. A language which is 'as poor as the feelings that are still close to the bones' but, at the same time, essential and almost sacred in its destitution, just as is the life that continues at that point to inhabit the body.

The body as a link between the present and the actual occurrence of the trauma

This body, displayed immediately with no mediation, defines the victim's identity and shows how far he or she has travelled in the process of destruction. It is also that body which designates the victim as such – as in the case of the Tutsi, in whom the perpetrators of genocide thought they could distinguish the characteristics that they insisted on attributing to them, just as the Nazis attempted to define a Jewish 'type', before circumcision made their task easier. Also, it is often the body that for a long time afterwards continues to bear the more or less visible marks of the physical abuse that was inflicted on it.

Revérien Rurangwa, a survivor of the genocide perpetrated against the Tutsi in Rwanda, was 15 years old at the time. He has written a book about what he underwent, one chapter of which is devoted to the body; it carries the title 'Dare to look me in the face'. 'Every morning, the same torture. The torture of the mirror.' Hideously mutilated, the young man describes that confrontation with a face that he no longer recognises as his own. What is he to do with that face, which he so much wants to wipe out? Indeed, is it really the face that he wants to wipe out or what it reminds him of – the most terrifying of moments?

He recalls images from a documentary dating from 1994, in which a mutilated child is sitting beside a dead woman. 'That absolutely stunned child is me. I am 15, but it looks as though I am only 8 years old.' It is difficult to connect with what he felt at that point since everything was experienced in terms of terror and of being far away from oneself. All that remains is the look in his eyes – or rather in his eye, his huge black eye, the only eye he has left because his other one had been ripped out.

It was through his attempt at getting to grips with that face of his that Revérien Rurangwa shaped his identity as a survivor. He refused cosmetic surgery, preferring to keep on his body the marks of the evil that had been done to him. A duty to remember, in which the body becomes a commemorative stela, showing to other people that the person concerned was the victim of genocide. The body is thus no longer simply that of the individual; it becomes a group body that carries with it some of the scars of the suffering inflicted upon the members of that group. As we read those pages, we come to realise the extent to which the duty to remain faithful to his own people weighs heavily on the young man's sense of identity and is an obstacle to his future: in a cry of despair, he wonders whether any woman could ever be attracted to such a scarred and disfigured man as he now is.

Grass has grown over the roads that lead to the houses that were set on fire, the churches have been cleansed of the blood of the victims, all trace of the genocide is disappearing. By staying the way he is, the victim rebels against the work of time and devotes himself to carrying time within himself. Against the erasing of the past, he offers himself as a witness – a martyr, in the strict sense of the word.

With the risk of collapsing into a state of melancholia that nothing will ever be able to contain.

With the risk of becoming the very person that the torturer had wanted to shape – a human being with his face and his soul slashed by a machete, someone who refuses to be part of human time once more, in order to remain in the no man's land of a survival that is not yet the life of human beings.

References

Améry, J. (1980) *At the Mind's Limits: Contemplations by a Survivor on Auschwitz and its Realities* (tran. S. and S. Rosenfeld), Bloomington, USA: Indiana University Press.

Antelme, R. ([1947] 1993) *The Human Race* (trans. J. Haight and A. Mahler), Marlboro, VT: Marlboro Press.

Delbo, C. ([1971] 1997) *The Measure of Our Days* (trans. R. Lamont), New Haven, CT: Yale University Press.

Freud, S. ([1914] 1957) 'On narcissism: an introduction', *Standard Edition*, vol. 14. London: The Hogarth Press, pp. 73–102.

Jurgenson, L. (2003) *L'Expérience Concentrationnaire est-elle Indicible?* Paris: Verdier.

Kestemberg, J. and Brenner, I. (1986) 'Le narcissisme comme moyen de survie', *Revue Française de Psychanalyse*, 6: 1393–1407.

Klemperer, V. (1975) *The Language of the Third Reich. LTI, Lingua Tertii Imperii: A Philologist's Notebook* (trans. M. Brady), London and New York: Continuum, 2006.

Rurangwa, R. (2006) *Genocide: My Stolen Rwanda* (trans. A. Brown), London: Reportage Press.

Shalamov, V. Ti ([1994] 2009) *Kolyma Tales* (trans. John Glad), London: Penguin.

Waintrater R. ([2003] 2009), *Sortir du Génocide: Témoignage et survivance*, Paris: Payot.

Waintrater R. (2010) 'Quand vivre est tout le sacré' in V. Altounian and J. Altounian (eds) *Memoires du Génocide Arménien: Héritage Traumatique et Travail Analytique*. Paris: Presses Universitaires de France.

Zaltzman, N. (1999) 'Homo sacer, l'homme tuable', in *La Résistance de l'Humain*, Paris: PUF.

8

THE BODY AND AIDS TRANSFORMED INTO A WORK OF ART BY HERVÉ GUIBERT

Anne Brun

Hervé Guibert was a French writer who died in 1991. When he realised that he had AIDS and that his death would not be long in coming, writing became for him a genuine means of survival. 'It is when I write that I am most alive' (1991: 144). 'When I am no longer writing, I am dying.' What were the issues facing that author in his creative work, accomplished in the context of a fatal illness at a time when triple therapy and antiretroviral drugs did not yet exist, so that such patients could not expect to live for much longer than 2 years? I shall show that the sources of this writer's creative process consisted of applying to his writing the survival strategies that aim at avoiding psychical death. This autobiographical work can teach us a great deal about the clinical aspects of psychical survival in extreme situations.

It was not AIDS that prompted Hervé Guibert to take up writing. Already an accomplished author and photographer who had had 13 books published by the time he was 34, he was highly thought of by those who were familiar with his work. It was, however, his last books, in which he wrote of his fight against AIDS, that made his name known to a much wider readership: in 1990, with *À l'Ami Qui ne M'a pas Sauvé la Vie* [*To the Friend Who Did Not Save My Life*] and in 1991, the year of his death, with *Le Protocole Compassionnel* [*The Compassioned Protocol*]. Several more works were published posthumously, including his logbook *Le Mausolée des Amants* [*The Lovers' Mausoleum*]. In the year that he died, Guibert directed a film about his illness, called *La Pudeur et l'Impudeur* [*Modesty and Immodesty*].

One feature of the intense media coverage of his book *À l'Ami Qui ne M'a pas Sauvé la Vie* – some 400,000 copies of which were sold in 4 years – was the scandal that resulted from Guibert's revelations about Michel Foucault: in the book, Guibert makes no secret of the fact that the philosopher, called Muzil in the book, died of AIDS. Guibert saw in him the image of what his own fate would be.

Without going into any detail about that media coverage, I shall explore the changes that AIDS brought about in Guibert's creative process and the role played by this corporeal style of writing in the context of his illness. Although, after he fell ill, Guibert did indeed give considerable importance to AIDS in his written work, those books were part of an ongoing literary project, the aim of which was to explore just how far one can go in writing about oneself. The thread that runs through all of his eclectic *oeuvre* is without doubt that autobiographical dimension – or, rather, auto-fictional dimension, because it is defined by the interplay between truth and complete invention, which is also characteristic of writing about AIDS.

Guibert described the entire collection of his work as the story of a body. It is indeed impossible to evoke simply the second series of his writings, devoted to the illness from which he was suffering, without at the same time thinking of the way in which, in his earlier work, he wrote of the sexual pleasure of the body and of homosexuality. When AIDS struck, that initial evocation of sexual pleasure in the body then moved towards a representation of the degeneration of his body that had become a martyr.

The literary works of Hervé Guibert (1955–1991) can be defined as a written and pictorial description of the body and they evolved in parallel with his AIDS-related illness towards a display of the degeneration of his body turned into that of a martyr. A psychoanalytical approach to his final autobiographical writings shows how – for a writer faced with the gradual decay of his body, the intrusion of new medical technologies and the certainty of his imminent end – the sources of the creative process consist of making use in his writing of survival strategies in order to avoid death. In this way, the writer/photographer, already in the grip of death, puts himself on show, and, paradoxically, kills himself in order to survive. He is destined to be the hero of his own story/history through the creation of a textual *corpus* created on the basis of the gradual destruction of his living body.

This writing of an 'extreme' body enables us to appreciate the function of creation in the context of a fatal illness. It can be seen as a re-situating in history of the body through 'the body of the work'. As though echoing the clinical features of AIDS, in Guibert's writings, the virus evokes a struggle against destructive archaic imagos and in particular reactivates a deadly body-to-body combat with the maternal imago, one of the sources of his creative process.

Guibert's literary work highlights some of the processes of survival that can be found in patients faced with 'extreme situations' of subjectivity (Brun 2013a), in various contexts of clinical encounters.

Writing of/about trauma

The author's display of his sick body, in both his writings and on film, has undoubtedly to do with an extreme form of aesthetics, one that challenges the frontier between art and reality. That kind of borderline aesthetics can be looked upon as heralding modern art – and especially the fine arts, which devote considerable space to bodies that are disfigured, mutilated, devitalised or tortured.

What is specific to Hervé Guibert, however, is undoubtedly the fact that the destruction of his body became the very source of the creative process at work in him. It was the very decomposition of his body that went hand-in-hand with the construction of 'the body of his work' (Anzieu 1981). At the source of the creative process lay the gradual deterioration of his living body that impelled him to create a textual *corpus* as a replacement.

> The body of an old man had taken possession of my body, that of a 35-year-old. It was probably the case that, as I lost my strength, I became much older than my father, who had just turned 70. I was 95 years old, like my great-aunt Suzanne, who was completely disabled…
>
> *(Guibert 1991: 12)*

Guibert stirs up in his readers feelings that are hardly bearable. The spectacle of the gradual deterioration of his sick body, all the more striking in that his face had retained its 'archangel'-like beauty, gives rise to stirrings of horror mingled with terror and fascination. The author speaks directly to us, pursuing us in our voyeurism, not to say sadism. He writes, for example: 'Can you bear a story like that, with all that blood? Does it excite you?' It is an extreme form of writing; the reader never stops wanting to put it aside but at the same time is faced with something like an obligation not to close his/her eyes, to continue to bear witness to the suffering that is in the author's body. The compassionate relationship between author and reader is tinted with a shared hatred – that of the ill author for the healthy reader and that of the reader for the author who inflicts such unbearable feelings on him/her.

In these books about AIDS, the body becomes the *locus* of all action, with the struggle against opportunistic diseases: PCP, toxoplasmosis, the cytomegalovirus attacking the patient's eyesight and which he chose as the title of his logbook while he was in hospital (Guibert 1992). The various treatments, accompanied by hope and disappointment, are one of the fundamental threads of the plot: *À l'Ami Qui Ne M'a Pas Sauvé La Vie* is, as it were, an account of the AZT treatment, and *Le Protocole Compassionnel* that of DDI. Each of these books is marked by a kind of race against time, in the hope that some new treatment might be discovered. Time starts getting out of control, and Guibert's writings give us a feeling of such urgency that we become almost breathless – an effect that is produced by the author's literary style: long sentences with little punctuation that carry the reader along at a furious pace, with no interruptions; the reader becomes dizzy as he/she reads these books, with their style that is close to a complete dismantling of feelings and images.

> Turner painted *Death on a Pale Horse*, last night I thought about that image again, it came back to me very precisely as it galloped along in all of its madness, I myself became that upturned body on the horse, with strips of flesh clinging to the bones, you almost want to scrape them clean once and for all, the living corpse bent down on that Fury as it charges along in the

> night, with its fur so warm and odorous, jolted about by its stampeding, a skeleton tied to the speeding horse, tearing through the storm, the foaming of the volcano, with an enormous hand that suddenly appears in the painting, a meat-beater hurled forward by the movement, destabilising the whole image. The ghost, in its skeleton nakedness, wears a diadem.
>
> *(Guibert 1991: 176)*

In his writing, Guibert conveys to his readers a similar feeling of seizing hold of the textual content; the reader too is dragged headlong towards catastrophe, with no possibility of resisting the momentum. At the same time, Guibert seizes hold, as it were, of his readers by addressing us directly in such a way that we feel that we are involved in the story: 'I like it when things go as directly as possible between my thoughts and yours, when matters of style do not prevent transfusion.' The reader therefore becomes transfused, contaminated by the text, just as the author explicitly expects a real transubstantiation with his readers. This is a kind of a vampiric reading in which the writer survives thanks to the new blood that his readers bring him. In a metaphorical way, Guibert assigns to his readers the task of developing the negatives:

> It is my soul that I am dissecting ... on it I do all sorts of tests, cross-section photographs, investigations via magnetic resonance, endoscopes, radioscopy, scans; I'll give you the negatives, and you can decipher them on the luminous plate of your sensitivity.
>
> *(Guibert 1991: 80–81)*

It is up to his readers to describe the author's experience by becoming a living mirror for him. One striking fact is that the author writes only about what is happening to his body (photographs, endoscopes, radioscopy, scans) without in the least mentioning his feelings. This is a style of writing that is trauma-based, a complete paralysis that is accompanied by his attempts to neutralise his emotions through the use of medical imagery, freezing of the affects, petrification – all of them survival strategies in extreme situations. What the narrator is transfusing into the reader is the trauma of AIDS – he leaves it up to us to feel the sheer horror of that illness, helplessness, repulsion and distress. In other words, the reader is obliged to feel what Guibert cannot feel in himself – what he can no longer allow himself to feel, for otherwise he would fall into the deepest despair of all. In our clinical work with patients who have AIDS, we often encounter that kind of defensive manoeuvre: they cut themselves off from their mental life, avoid thinking and neutralise their affects in order to protect themselves against unbearable pain and suffering. In their counter-transference, echoing this, therapists may find themselves in the grip of a white-out as regards their thinking and of a neutralisation of their feelings; they may be contaminated by that state of psychical death, a decathexis that is an effect of the death drive or of the patient's experience of collapsing (Brun 2013a).

In other words, the writer, faced with the inhumanity of the medical approach, appeals to the reader's sensitivity as though the latter were in a position to carry the writer's affects, to filter his emotions and to guarantee that any lost meanings will be found again. We can thus begin to see how vital and urgent it is to read Guibert's writings and to stay by his side as he walks along the hospital corridors. Guibert said quite clearly that he felt 'comforted' by the fact that his first AIDS-related book had met with such success – he 'carried that inside [himself] like a talisman that would protect [him] from death and exorcize [him]' (Guibert 1991: 195). He dedicated *Le Protocole Compassionnel* to all those who had written to him about *À l'Ami Qui ne M'a pas Sauvé la Vie*. 'I was overwhelmed by every single one of your letters,' he wrote. There is probably no better way of describing how those letters put Guibert back in touch with his own emotions, as it were.

> In fact, I wrote a letter which was immediately telefaxed into the hearts of 100,000 people, it's extraordinary. I am at present writing them another letter. I'm writing to you.
>
> *(op. cit.: 141)*

The fantasy of transubstantiation actually acquires some degree of consistency – indeed, a young female doctor tries to persuade Guibert to accept blood and medulla from her (op. cit.: 205)! In this way, the writer succeeded in mobilising to an incredible extent a fantasy of actually triumphing over death through his writing and by stimulating his readers to such a degree – as though life were a novel. Therein lies another dimension of Guibert's writing – the fictionalisation, as it were, of his suffering, such that turning it into a story enables some degree of distantiation: 'It is when what I write becomes like a diary that my impression of fiction is at its strongest' (op. cit.: 103).

When all is said and done, the title *To The Friend Who Did Not Save My Life* applies to the book itself: it was unable to save its author. 'A written work is the exorcism of powerlessness. At the same time, an unavoidable illness is the height of powerlessness' (Guibert 1991: 265).

Writing: an 'extreme body'

Creation is an attempt both at getting to grips with a body over which the individual has no longer any control and an attempt at distancing him/herself with respect to that body which has indeed turned into a 'foreign' body. All books about AIDS have to do with some degree of radical separation between body and mind, an experience of complete alienation with respect to the body. Guibert describes the fundamental experience of facing up each morning to his nakedness in the mirror, that of someone who seems to be a stranger:

> There was never a day in which I failed to discover some new and disturbing streak, a new lack of flesh on the frame, ... now the bone seemed to

> emerge from the skin, on its very surface like those little flat islands on the surface of the sea. My skin ebbed back behind the bone, which pushed it …. I cannot say that I felt any kind of pity for that guy, it depended on how I was feeling, from time to time I have the impression that he'll pull through because, after all, some people did manage to come back from Auschwitz. At other times, I can see that he is doomed, he's on the way to his grave, inevitably.
>
> *(Guibert 1991: 18–19)*

The words 'that guy' indicate the alienation of the first-person dimension (the 'I'), which has lost its image in the mirror. The author makes use of a style of writing that functions as a mirror in order to reappropriate his own body image, in order to see himself through the imagined eyes of his readers. In Guibert's own words, he made quite an exhibition of his 'corpse', his 'remains', his 'skeleton' – to the extent of causing a scandal, for example, when in the course of some shows, he exhibited his naked and emaciated body. Making such a huge exhibition of himself was perhaps his way of reversing the shame that he felt. Showing himself off like that amounted to another kind of survival strategy, in which what was at stake was the ability to put up with dereliction by imposing it on other people, and this with a twofold objective: that of himself provoking the repulsion that frightened him, and that of gaining the sympathy of other people.

Given the extreme desexualisation of the body, writing would seem to be one last attempt at not giving in to the extinguishing of everything that is drive-related, and perhaps even an attempt at erotogenisation of his own body. This is what Guibert wrote in *Le Protocole Compassionnel*, which bears witness to the fact that, after the phase in which his body deteriorated catastrophically, he was again feeling better: 'I was alive again. I was writing again. I was getting hard-ons again' (Guibert 1991: 64).

This was not a return to any kind of sexuality, henceforth felt to be impossible; Guibert wrote that he still loved Vincent but that touching his body hardly awakened anything at all in him :

> I knew his body off by heart. It had become imprinted inside my fingers, I didn't need it any more in actual reality.
>
> *(op. cit.: 165)*

By contrast, he describes his daily physical exercises as being a source of pleasure – the pleasure found in re-experiencing sensori-motor functions and in the very movement of writing by his body. Instead of letting himself fall into despair and resignation when faced with the degeneration of his body, he attempted some degree of re-integration with respect to the death drive, with the help of sensori-motor functions that were not restricted to gymnastic movements – they included the bodily movement brought about by writing, which helped him to 'get back on his feet': 'I am a beetle lying on its back, its shell, and struggling to get its feet back on the ground. I'm struggling too. Oh my God, what a beautiful struggle' (op. cit.: 175).

Writing also helped him to eroticise his relationship with his doctor, a woman. He describes the pleasure that he felt when she took off his socks and undressed him. This was not a matter of Guibert suddenly becoming heterosexual(!), but he seemed to find in that relationship a maternal quality, with the possibility of erotogenising his body. On the back cover of *Le Protocole Compassionnel*, we read: 'With each medical examination, a strange relationship will be set up between that very beautiful woman and the narrator. A relationship that is perhaps close to love, who knows.'

Fiction is called upon to reawaken the drives in a body that had become a walking corpse. The author thinks of his writings as being also a way of fighting against AIDS: 'That diary was also intended to be the diary of a war' (Guibert 1992: 18). The body becomes both the *locus* of action and the body of the text, with its struggle against opportunistic ailments: the various treatments, accompanied by hopes and disappointments, are the main thread that runs through the whole plot, with on each occasion a race against time in the hope that some new treatment will be discovered. The fight against AIDS often takes the form of violence turned against the medical and nursing team, experienced as aggressors; the author's writing becomes a tract driven by a murderous and destructive anger, an imprecation that sometimes was so extreme that it became exhilarating[1] – describing the doctors, for example, as commandos who cut the throats of pigs, pointing out:

> the extent to which the body … thrown into the channels of medicine, loses all identity and is no more than a packet of flesh, with no will-power, carted about here and there, hardly even a number, a name that gets put through the administrative mill, bled of all history and dignity.
>
> *(Guibert, 1991, p. 32)*

Writing is therefore a struggle – against the de-humanisation, de-entification and desexualisation of a body that is given over to chemical prostheses: the author's works can be seen as the re-historicising of a body that has lost all subjectivity, and as an attempt at subjective re-appropriation when faced with the dehumanising element that comes into play when medicalisation becomes extreme. Guibert does not hesitate to include medical analyses in his narrative, as though trying, by adopting the discourse of his doctors, to recover some control over his sick body through his writing:

> The most recent analyses, dated 18 November, say that I have 384 T4; a male in good health has between 500 and 2,000 of these. T4 are those elements of the leucocytes that the AIDS virus attacks first, thereby gradually weakening the immunological defences.
>
> *(Guibert 1990: 13)*

This kind of writing corresponds first of all to an attempt at making what is perceived meaningful: when faced with an explosion of body-related perceptions and with the dismantling of the body and the feelings to which it gives rise, the writer has to re-appropriate and structure those various sense impressions. Through its figurative function, this style of writing enables forms to be created in order to fight against anxiety relating to death and to the disappearing of the self by making visible, audible and able to be put into words what lies somewhere in the realm of the intolerable and unintelligible. This is not a quest for some meaning or other; it simply makes sense data representable in order not to fall into a meaningless void. The writer bears witness to this when he describes his writing as similar to X-ray photographs that have to be deciphered by the reader who, in a way, is asked to make meaningful the author's de-subjectivising experiences.

It is an attempt at recording in writing what cannot be thought about or put into words; a text which, as the author puts it, is 'the only way to forget' (Guibert 1991: 54). These paradoxes may to some extent become clearer when compared to writings about the Shoah. Guibert often refers to that genocide, comparing himself to someone deported to Auschwitz. Recording the traumatism in collective memory enables it to be erased; in Freudian terms, the transcription of unthinkable and irrepresentable perceptual residues into representations enables some image of what cannot be represented to be shared with other human beings. Horror must be shared with other people before one can liberate oneself of it.

Writing as a struggle against a primitive maternal imago reincarnated through the virus

In Guibert's literary work, the AIDS virus evokes a struggle against destructive archaic imagos and reactivates, as it were, a deadly body-to-body combat with the maternal imago. At the beginning of his *Diary*, the author writes about his birth: his mother told him that the 9 months during which she was pregnant with him were 'the worst in her whole life'.

> It was my father who had forced her to have a baby … and all through those nine months her hysterical wish was to get rid of me. She let herself fall down the stairs in order to abort me. When at last they took me out of her womb, she begged: 'Let's hope he's dead! Let's hope he's stillborn!' 'Then I saw you,' she said, 'all tiny and naked, miserable, lying on a table – and I screamed: Look out! He's going to fall off…!'.
>
> *(Guibert 1991: 79)*

Hervé Guibert reported this story about his mother long before he discovered that he had AIDS, but one cannot help feeling that AIDS seemed to reactualise what he was destined for from birth onwards – death – as though his illness gave concrete expression to his mother's death-wish concerning him.

In order to ward off that threat of death, the only solution that the writer/photographer had was to put himself on show, already in the grip of death, and to transpose that primary catastrophe into the aesthetic sphere. Guibert therefore filmed himself committing suicide, anticipating, announcing and surviving that suicide through his literary work. Another strategy of psychical survival: inflicting death on oneself, in this case in an anticipatory manner, the better to keep it at bay – killing oneself in order to survive.

Guibert's fight against AIDS echoed his struggle against a primitive maternal imago that threatened him with disintegration – one that could coincide with the presence of the destructive virus. In our clinical work, the coalescence between the virus and a destructive imago is a very frequent occurrence. One of my patients, a homosexual drag artist, had a somatic breakdown when his mother rejected him and refused to have any more to do with him. The virus had become a death-dealing mother, just at the point where his health had dramatically deteriorated. When, in the course of his therapy, we did some work on his maternal imago – to differentiate it from the virus (Brun 2013b) – his somatic well-being improved significantly.

I shall let Guibert have the last word.

> Yes, I can put it down in writing – and that's what my madness probably is: I care more about my book than about my life. I would not give up my book in order to preserve my life – that will be the most difficult thing for people to believe and to make them understand.
>
> *(Guibert 1990: 257)*

It is his books that have made Hervé Guibert immortal, at the cost of sacrificing his living body, transmuted into a work of art. In his final writings, the destruction of his body becomes the very source of his creative process: the very decomposition of his body goes hand in hand with the construction of the *corpus* of his work. AIDS gradually directed Guibert's literary work towards opening up to the suffering that all human beings have to confront, a suffering in which his readers can share. In his final written work, one of the functions of writing consists in implementing survival strategies in order to avoid psychical death. The psychoanalytical approach to his *oeuvre* has enabled us to highlight some survival processes that we find in patients confronted with 'extreme situations' of subjectivity, such as a fatal illness which may, paradoxically, turn out to be a source of creation.

Note

1 That element of imprecation reminds us of Thomas Bernhard's writings; Hervé Guibert discovered these with enthusiasm, just as he was falling ill. In Thomas Bernhard's case, part of the creative process of writing comes from the projective reversal of primordial distress into an intense and provocative jubilation, which he was able to share with his readers (Brun 2012).

References

Anzieu, D. (1981) *Le Corps de l'Œuvre.* Paris: Gallimard.
Brun, A. (2013a) 'Thomas Bernhard, une écriture de la survie', in A. Brun and B. Chouvier (eds). *L'Archaïque : Création et Psychanalyse.* Paris: Armand Colin.
Brun, A. (2013b) 'A clinical exploration of fetishism and primary identification', *Canadian Journal of Psychoanalysis*, 21(2): 123–144.
Guibert, H. (1990) *À l'Ami Qui ne M'a pas Sauvé la Vie.* Paris: Gallimard. [*To The Friend Who Did Not Save My Life.* (trans. L. Cloverdale). New York: High Risk Books, 1993.]
Guibert, H. (1991) *Le Protocole Compassionnel.* Paris: Gallimard.
Guibert, H. (1992) *Cytomégalovirus.* Paris: Seuil.
Guibert, H. (2001) *Le Mausolée des Amants.* Paris: Gallimard.

9

THE 'COMPOSITE BODY' IN CONTEMPORARY ART

Catherine Desprats Péquignot

In the 1960s, male and female artists associated with the *body art* movement in the United States and with its European counterpart, *l'Art Corporel*, began to use the body as both the material and the site for questioning their artistic practice. From this movement emerged a number of projects highlighting what we could call the 'composite body', which foregrounds contemporary ideas and dreams of 'the new body', the body of the future. These works generally fall into two categories.

On the one hand, we see visual depiction of human figures that are a combination of sexes and genders. These bodies are presented to the spectator as neither male nor female, but also as both male and female, as transsexual or transgender. They represent an ideal or a dream of the 'trans' body: a body that blurs the limits and transgresses the differences between sexed bodies, thus destroying the normative binary; a body modelled on anatomical hermaphroditism, transsexualism and transvestitism. In this category, we could cite the works of the British painter Jenny Saville, for example her painting *Passage* (2004), or the androgynous creations of the American artist Matthew Barney.

On the other hand, we have the works of mostly female artists, who often use their own body to figure and symbolise a certain idea of femininity, one that brings opposites together in an image of bi-sexed wholeness: the ancient mother goddess. In this case, the ideal or dream seems to be a rediscovery, within the woman's own body or sex, of a unified androgynous matrix, whose traces have been preserved in mythology and in certain visual representations of 'composite bodies'. A good example of this is the work of the American performance artist Carolee Schneemann, which I discuss in more detail below.

These ideals and contemporary dreams are framed by the same set of fantasies that have underpinned the traditional and ancestral uses of visual and discursive imagery from which 'composite bodies' draw their inspiration. This concerns, for example, the imaginary and symbolic figure of the snake, which features heavily in

Carolee Schneemann's work; I will use this image to examine the fantasies at work in the contemporary approach to the body and to its image as the material site of identity, following the equivalence made between the body/image and the ego.

Carolee Schneemann: the 'composite body' and the snake symbol

In the case of Carolee Schneemann, one of the real pioneers of body art, the staging of the artist's own naked body and sex is supported and legitimised by (1) a certain mystique of the uterine matrix, its cosmic energy and generative force; (2) the idea of 'primal' femininity with an androgynous character and powers, which transcends sexual and gender divisions, and (3) by a feminist discourse about the female body, sex and 'interior space' Schneemann's work wants to valorise and celebrate. One of the ways in which this valorisation and celebration is staged is by associating the female body and sex with the symbol of the snake. This has been part of Schneemann's research into the 'vulvic space', which she began in the 1960s.

In some of the photographs featured in her 1963 work *Eye Body (36 Transformative Actions)* Schneemann appears naked, surrounded by serpent-like ropes, with garden snakes crawling on her stomach and torso. The artist claims that only after she had created the piece, she learned about the serpent being an attribute of ancient goddesses, such as the Minoan Snake Goddess from 1600 BC, to which she refers. This well-known symbol is of agricultural fertility and a personification of Mother Earth holding snakes in her raised hands.

Interior Scroll, which was performed in the United States first in 1975 and then again in 1977, also uses the symbol of the snake, this time in the form of a scroll of paper, which the artist draws out of her vagina, treating it as a snake/phallus, and from which she reads out feminist texts. She writes about the vagina: '[I saw the vagina as] a translucent chamber of which the serpent was an outward model: enlivened by its passage from the visible to the invisible, a spiraled coil ringed with the shape of desire and generative mysteries, attributes of both female and male sexual powers' (Schneemann 1979).

What Schneemann is trying to achieve by associating the female body with the serpent as a symbol of the earliest times, of the 'cosmic energy of the female uterus, which protects and nourishes the embryo', is to create a figure of primordial femininity that precedes any division and separation, any sexual and gender duality. We find this 'two-sided' symbol (of both the vulva and the phallus) again and again in Schneemann's work, for example in the motif of the umbrella. The open or closed umbrella evokes the idea of both the vagina-uterus and the penis. In *Fresh Blood* (1980), the artist dances with a transparent umbrella (representing a translucent uterus), while reciting: 'umbrella cunt, umbrella *both cunt and cock* ... cunt cock ... cunt clasping cock'. She connects the cunt/cock umbrella with the paper scroll which she had drawn out of her vagina in *Interior Scroll* and which she associates with the serpent. The scroll/serpent is therefore a symbol of the cunt/cock and of the cock/cunt, a figure of the androgynous character of femininity, abolishing the differences or the binary opposites of the sexes and the genders assigned to them.

The snake: a 'two-sided' symbol of masculinity and femininity

The snake as a symbol of the genitalia has been known to all cultures since antiquity. This 'two-sided' figure may also symbolise the uterus or the vulva (in this case it is represented in the form of a circle or a lozenge); however, most often it symbolises the phallic dimension attributed to penile erection: for example, the snakes in the hands of the Minoan Goddess symbolise her phallic dimension. On the one side, the snake is associated with the Earth and the lunar cycle (and via the latter with the menstrual cycle), but also with renewal and fertility – just like the symbol of the phallus to which it is connected, both sharing the values of fertility, renewal, protection and power.

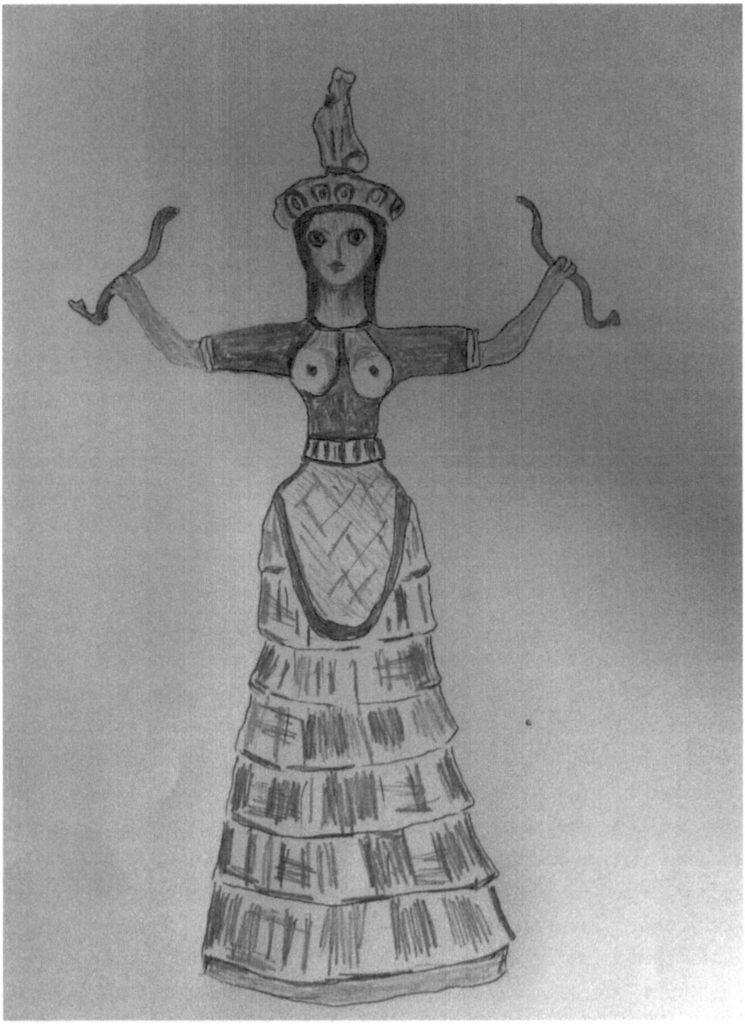

FIGURE 9.1 Pencil drawing, Minoan Goddess, Crete

Like some other animals, the serpent is a metaphor for both desire and fear, for danger and hope. Its moulting and regeneration can represent the revival of fertility; when standing tall and moulting, it can signify phallic erection and its renewal – like the Sphinx who is reborn from the ashes. The snake's bite is an analogy of coitus and penetration. In many legends the snake explains the origins of blood in female defloration and menstruation. As we are reminded by Schneemann's performance, which combines ancient legend with a common fantasy, we can also imagine it coiled up in the vagina or the uterus – it can then bite and harm the penis, or even bite it off and swallow it, when the latter dares to enter the snake's uterine lair during sexual intercourse.

The two-sided symbol of the snake therefore combines masculinity and femininity: on the male side, it can take on the value of a phallic symbol, while on the female side it can represent the powers of the female or maternal belly – fertility and regeneration, but also their very opposite: destruction and devouring. With its gaping mouth, expandable jaws, teeth or fangs, with its ability to attack and swallow its prey whole and alive, expanding its body to absorb it, the snake in fact concentrates the anxieties, fears and fantasies of the 'toothed vagina', of the voracious uterus, of the female belly with its consuming sexual appetite, which likes to suck in and swallow the penis through its vaginal mouth.

Should we therefore be surprised to find the snake associated with the Judeo-Christian myth of the 'first woman' from the biblical story of Genesis – not only Eve, but also Lilith, whom some of the traditions and narratives consider Adam's first companion. Neither male nor female, but an androgynous figure uniting the opposites, Lilith represents the archaic mother goddess or a night demon supposedly able to assume the form of a snake. According to one version, Adam repudiated Lilith and she became the tempting serpent in order to get her revenge, seducing Eve in the Garden of Eden. This is why she is sometimes recognised in the figure of the female-headed snake, or a snake with a female head and bust. The female-headed snake pictured in the Garden of Eden would therefore give visual form to a certain imaginary of the body and would symbolise the first woman's androgynous femininity – not only concerning Lilith, but also Eve, since the snake's female head seems to be her double or her mirror image.

Numerous representations of the tempting snake in the scene of the original sin give it this female head and sometimes also a female bust. In some of them, the snake's body resembles a lizard, but more often, the head and the bust, or the head alone, lengthen into a giant snake's tail wrapped around the Tree of Knowledge – for example in Michelangelo's paintings on the ceiling of the Sistine Chapel in Vatican or on portraits in the Notre-Dame Cathedral in Paris.

Here too we see the phallic and androgynous dimension of the snake symbol, representing the androgynous femininity of the 'first woman'. It also reminds us of the original androgyny attributed by different traditions and ancient religions to primordial beings, as it has been transmitted to us by the myths and legends of a number of different cultures. We often see these male and female aspects of the mother goddesses represented visually: sometimes they are depicted as half-women,

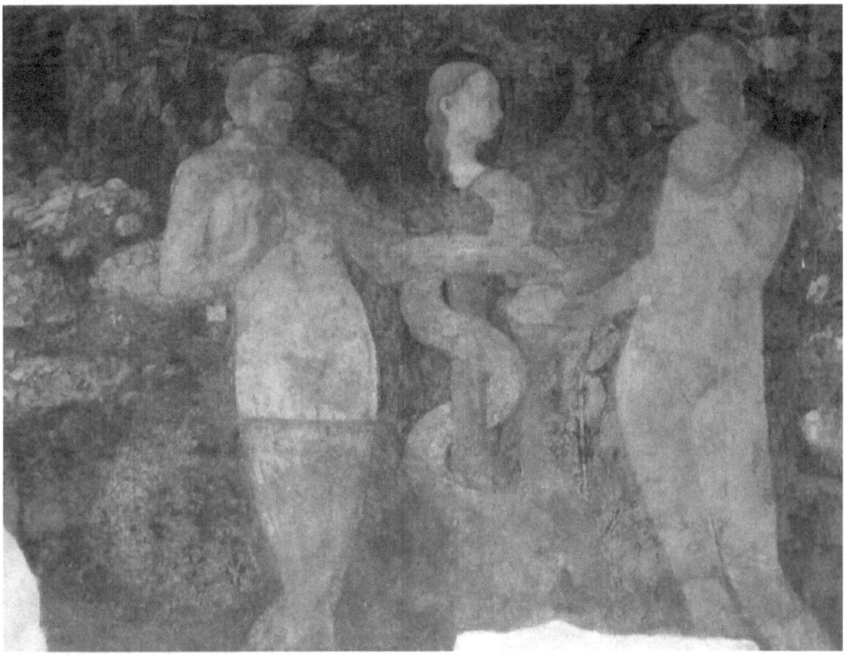

FIGURE 9.2 Chiostro Verde, the Church of Santa Maria Novella, Florence

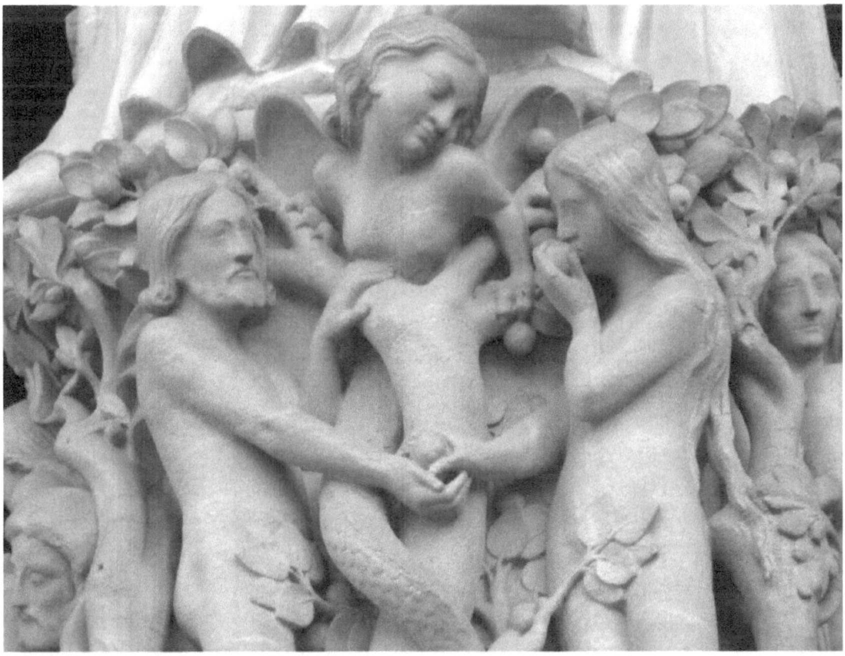

FIGURE 9.3 Fragment of the Portal of the Virgin, the Notre-Dame Cathedral, Paris

half-snakes; sometimes they are endowed with a penis, such as in the case of the so-called 'bearded Aphrodite' (500–400 BC). To borrow an example from Freud, the Egyptian maternal divinity Mut also had a female body and breasts, but it was represented with an erect penis. Freud was very interested in this 'psychological riddle' – how can we explain the fact that human fantasy attributes this antinomic sign of 'male potency' to a figure representing the 'essence of a mother'? This figure of motherhood is not endowed with simply a flaccid penis, but with 'masculine power', i.e. with the phallic value of an erected penis, of the 'stiff rod' of might and power, of the force assigned to the staff which, in the story of Moses, too, could transform into a snake.

The image of a 'total maternal being'

The imaginary structure of the female/maternal body as a 'total being' has therefore existed and been fantasised about since antiquity. This structure pays no heed to the difference of the sexes, which are instead combined in a 'totality'; its strength and power are represented by phallic symbols that may be associated with bodies both 'feminine' and 'masculine'. In this sense, these primordial women/mothers, the androgynous mother goddesses bearing a phallus – whether the latter is visually depicted as an erect member, a serpent, a stick, or otherwise – all represent the 'phallic mother'. In other words, they figure the power, strength and force of a 'total maternal being', one that is beyond difference, neither male nor female, and both at the same time. They represent its dream and its ancient fantasy. They are both a 'mythological' and visual embodiment of the 'Total-Mother' (*Toute Mère*) of childhood memory, of infantile desire and love – the 'total' or 'phallic mother' so splendidly represented by Louise Bourgeois' monstrous spiders, particularly the one she aptly entitled *Maman*.

The fantasy and the belief in the 'phallic mother' are forged from the traces of the archaic maternal imago – 'the imago of the maternal breast which is no breast at all' as Lacan had already suggested in 1938.– i.e., from the survival, within our imagination, of the 'ancient mother', of a total maternal being. This phallic mother leaves indelible traces on the mental life of the child, regardless of whether it is a boy or a girl. We could in fact imagine that this primordial form of the maternal imago, the imago of the 'maternal breast that dominates all human life' (Lacan 1938) and is transformed by the Oedipus complex, with the castration complex as its integral part and the phallic phase its corresponding stage, contributes to the creation of the 'infantile theory of the maternal phallus' (Freud 1910) and the construction of the 'phallic mother'. This happens either before or once the mother's 'castration' has been discovered or, as we could say, when the child finds out that the mother is not 'complete' – that she is lacking and desires something she does not have. To the child, this lack becomes represented by the bodily presence or absence of a single element. This difference is played out in language, in what the child hears within the family and the culture at large, and is part of the vision that governs sex and gender assignment since birth – it's a girl, it's a boy – regardless of what the real sex may be.

The discovery of the mother's 'castration' leads to her fall from the position of the 'Total Mother'. She becomes a woman with 'nothing left', as Louise Bourgeois puts it. Her sculptures castrate the 'very strong mother' of her childhood memories, reducing her to a 'poor woman' – fallen, disarmed, helpless and powerless. The fantasy of the 'phallic mother', of her power and strength, of the 'masculine power of the maternal being' (Freud) becomes associated with a nostalgia for a paradise lost – such as the imago of the maternal breast – i.e. for a primordial, mythical time, prior to any separation or division, a time before any loss, lack and otherness. A fantasy of absorption and unity, of completeness that precedes any division, separation, dis-section or 'sex-ion'. A nostalgia for the 'Total Mother', for the completeness of the 'earliest times', which for Carolee Schneemann is symbolised by the Minoan Snake Goddess and which Louise Bourgeois represents in all its power and strength by the figure of the spider – an animal that Freud and Abraham also considered to symbolise the 'phallic mother'.

Pursuing this line of inquiry further, we could ask whether the 'composite bodies' of modern art do not again stage the primordial and 'whole' bodies of the myths of origin, bodies which belong to a time before any division, including sexual and gender division, before differentiation and otherness. These 'composite bodies' would be modeled on traditional fantasies; they would be objectifications of an imago, but at the same time also new and modern solutions to the ancient riddles of sexuality, otherness, loss and desire.

Looking at the contemporary approaches to the body and the discourses governing the body and body image as sites of the materialisation of identity, of a 'this is me', based on the equation made between 'my body' and 'my self', we may also wonder if these 'composite bodies', which are often offered to us as ideals potentially attainable through the latest medical technologies, do not represent forms of wish-fulfillment. From this perspective, they would be fuelled by the desire for 'wholeness' which unfolds against the background of loss and aims to establish an equivalence or an identity (*idem* meaning 'the same') between the self (or the self-image) and the primordial object – the always already lost object known in psychoanalysis as 'the breast'.

Freud articulates this equivalence or identity as: 'I am the breast'. Therefore – and I will end with this question – aren't the 'composite bodies' that modern art wants to show us, that it wants us to enjoy, primarily organised around the 'imago of the maternal breast'? These anachronistic, infantile bodies, bodies of nostalgia and fantasy, shaped by the equivalence between 'the breast' (imago/totality) = self = body/body image, are they not the same bodies that many subjects seek to transform into reality by medical and surgical means? And are we so far from the imago of the 'breast', from the androgynous mother goddess and the 'primordial' beings of mythological tales, when we look at other present-day forms of this wholeness, of the 'composite body' becoming flesh? For the very first time in 2008, an American transsexual (who had undergone female-to-male reassignment surgery, but had kept his uterus) gave birth to a child.

Bibliography

Desprats-Péquignot, C. (2009) 'Le rêve d'un nouveau corps', In *Le Corps Contemporain: Creation et Faits de Culture*, Paris: L'Harmattan, 13–27.

Desprats-Péquignot, C. (2010) 'Sexes et genres de mort en deuil: Louise Bourgeois', In *Champ Psychosomatique*, 58: 199–221.

Freud, S. (1910) 'Leonardo da Vinci and a memory of his childhood', in J. Strachey (ed.) (1957) *The Standard Edition of the Complete Psychological Works of Sigmund Freud,* Volume XI, London: The Hogarth Press & The Institute of Psycho-analysis, 63–137.

Lacan, J. ([1938] 2001) 'Les complexes familiaux dans la formation de l'individu', in *Autres Ecrits*, Paris: Seuil, 23–84.

Le Long, D. (ed.) (2000) *Louise Bourgeois: Destruction du Père – Reconstruction du Père – Ecrits et Entretiens 1923–2000*, London: Violette Editions.

O'Reilly, S. (2009) *The Body in Contemporary Art*, London: Thames & Hudson Ltd.

Schneemann, C. (1979) *More Than Meat Joy: Complete Performance Works & Selected Writings*, Kingston: McPherson & Co.

10

THE MULTIPLE BODIES OF MICHAEL JACKSON

A paradigm for understanding postmodern society?

Silke Schauder

Neverending change

A planetary phenomenon, *Bambi*, *Jacko the Wacko*, Michael Jackson is a most fascinating study object for postmodern philosophy, gender studies and modern psychoanalysis.[1] As we showed in our former findings (Schauder, 2009, 2011a, b, 2013),[2] Jackson exemplifies the failure of adolescence : instead of a maturative crisis that comprises the mourning of childhood and the loss of the parental ideals, he aims neither in his life nor in his *oeuvre* at a construction of a stable identity opening to the possibilites of adulthood, i.e. sexuation, choice of a mate and a coherent life project. Instead, Jackson's artistic gesture is defined by undefinability, uncertainty and permanent change.[3]

In this permanent change, it is not the result, but the change itself, the never-ending transformation, that seems essential to him (Fisher, 2009).[4] Artistically, the theme of transformation is brilliantly worked through in his video clips where transformation and change take a very sophisticated part, i.e. in *Black or White* where the boundaries between humans and animals, man and woman and different cultures and places are torn down. Featuring the first and most famous morphing scene ever realised in a video, Michael changes into a black panther and back again. In the final sequence, several faces from all over the world blend one into the other, stating and emphasising that our humankind is *one*.

A more playful type of change takes place in the clips *Speed Demon* and *Leave Me Alone* where MJ shifts between reality and fiction, travelling through painted landscapes. *Speed Demon* depicts plastilin figures that turn into real people and back again and Michael having a dance contest with a rabbit named *Spike* which is actually his *alter ego*. In the clip *Remember the Time*, Michael morphs from dust into a golden figure and then into a sublime dancer and then turns back into dust.[5]

The best known metamorphosis takes place in the clip *Thriller*, where young Michael turns, under the pressure of his unassumed sex drive and a full moon, into a terrifying werewolf thus realising a blend between animal and man.[6] In our analysis of Michael Jackson's *Thriller* video (Schauder, 2011b, 2013), we articulated the werewolf myth to a discussion of adolescent metamorphosis. Through his self-fiction linking cinematographic references to myth and science fiction, Jackson shows, in a radical and transgressive postmodern gesture, the apparent absurdity of such oppositions as man-woman, angel-demon, human-animal, living-dead, reality-fiction. These mere pairings whose structuring power he shatters are constantly blended one into another, in order to replay the metamorphosis of adolescence, which is here marked by a tragic negativity. Thus, the potential reversibility of change and the artistically created illusion of permanent transformability abolishes the principle of stability inherent to the main definitions of identity. It is that shiver, that never-ending blur of boundaries that makes MJ's art so appealing, because it is firmly rooted in infantile fantasies of omnipotency. As unconditional fans, we all admire Michael Jackson so much and our emotional implication, grossly irrational, is so strong *because* he visualises in his art our own fantasies about invulnerability, immortality and omnipotence. The total power and megalomaniac features that are displayed for instance in the self-advertising clip *Brace Yourself* satisfy our own repressed ideas of grandiosity, thoroughly fed by music titles such as *Unbreakable* or *Invincible*.

Forever young

The fantasies of being forever young, of eternal life and of unlimited self are frequently found in psychosis as well as in the fantasies that underly the creativity of great artists. Jackson cumulates all these fantasies when, for instance, while visiting a shop he admires a pharaoh's sarcophagus made of gold and covered with precious stones. Martin Bashir asks him: 'Do you want to be buried in this?' Michael answers: 'I won't die; I will live forever'.[7]

On the level of bodily changes, he underwent a stupendous amount of plastic surgery in order to constantly change his face in shape and colour. We shall remember that Rodin, the modern French sculptor and one of the greatest portraitists, said: 'Each face is a forced space', which means one can't change all of its parameters all the time without losing, in the end, the face itself. Throughout the years, Michael Jackson *did* lose his face, abolishing all resemblance with himself, with his relatives and, in the end, with mankind. In his last years, he could only ressemble the *concept*, the *brand Michael Jackson* he had created himself, coming closer in appearance to a cyborg than to a human being. And brutally resiliating the contract of mutual recognition and human intimacy that the French philosopher Emmanuel Levinas (1995)[8] attributes, in an ethical sense, to the human face.[9] The extreme violence of Michael Jackson's facial changes may be seen not only as a Promethean gesture of inventing himself in sheer *hubris* and virtualising his face as if it were to be designed like a *cartoon*,[10] but as an attack on the family ties that were ambiguous, if not unbearable for Michael Jackson.

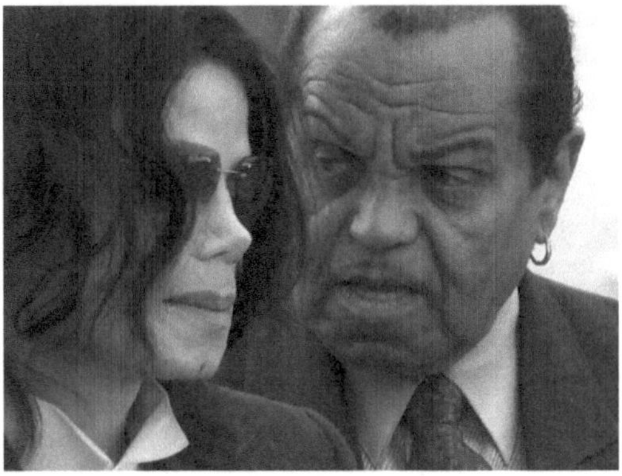

FIGURE 10.1 Joe and Michael Jackson

In particular, the strained relationship with his father put him in front of a true dilemma and a painful split of loyalty: on the one hand, Michael was heavily indebted to his father Joe who launched his career and managed the *Jackson 5*. On the other, Michael hated him for his cruelty,[11] his iron discipline and for denying his children their childhood.[12] As an adult, Michael Jackson had to struggle hard to establish his own artistic autonomy after leaving the *Jackson* 5 and his brothers to their much less successful musical career.[13]

Thus, the facial changes – the colour of the skin as well as the numerous changes of its characteristic Afro-American features – permitted Michael Jackson to step out of filiation, to quit his genealogy and to invent a new mankind after having torn down the boundaries that withheld the music of Afro-American artists to be played in the white man's music industry.[14] It is notable that the Afro-American community did not perceive Michael Jackson's facial and colour changes as a betrayal and stayed loyal fans, as if no change did actually happen (Laurent 2009a, b). Heavily rationalised as vitiligo, his colour changes were accompanied by a complete remodeling of his face shape, especially the nose that seemed to be of almost dysmorphophobian interest to Michael Jackson.[15] As he was bullied by his father as 'big nose' through childhood and adolescence,[16] erasing his nose was erasing the harmful words of his father and, through illusion of metonymy, erasing his father himself.[17]

Where do babies come from?[18]

The *hubris*[19] characteristic for his aesthetic project – to model a face that is no longer indebted to heritage – makes new ways for procreation and sets a new dynasty. Michael Jackson's interest in monstrosity, his fascination for Spielberg's *E.T.* and Lynch's *Elephant Man* may be linked to his own sense of abnormity, strangeness and a certain extraterritoriality that questions the boundary between human and non-human. Classically, the definition of a monster is 'one without descendance, the only one in his kind' (Beaune 2004). Truly, Michael Jackson was the only one of his kind and his strategies to assure fatherhood without sexual intercourse may be considered as leaving him potentially without descendants.[20] In a negation of alterity and difference, the existence of his three children seems only due to the godlike desire of their father, like in the Greek myth of Zeus who gives birth to Athena by opening his forehead or pulling her out of his thigh. The names Michael Jackson chose for them design them as genuine members of a royal dynasty the 'King of Pop' created himself: Michael Joseph 'Prince' Jackson Jr., born on 13 February, 1997, Paris Michael Katherine Jackson born on 3 April, 1998, their mother being his former nurse Debbie Rowe inseminated by his dermatologist[21]; 'Blanket', Prince Michael Jackson II was born to him by a surrogate mother on 21 February, 2002.[22]

It is notable that the two first children are named after his parents, Joseph and Katherine and that Michael's own name is narcissistically poured over all three, insuring his children are copies, *duplicata* or clones of himself.[23] Incestuous phantasies seem to stick Michael's name to Joseph's and Katherine's, introducing only a separation between Joseph and the family name by 'Prince' in the case of his first son and not between Katherine and Jackson in the case of his daughter. The numeration is somewhat erratic and lacking continuity – his first son is 'Jr.', referring implicitly to an unnamed 'Sr.', his father or Michael himself, his second son is '*II*', referring to a hypothetical '*I*', his eldest son or Michael himself. In any case, origin and reference are not clear and as shaky as often found in psychosis.

To moonwalk or not to moonwalk...

The *hubris syndrome* is present as well in several artistic inventions of Michael Jackson, i.e. the *moonwalk* in *Billy Jean* and the *lean* in *Smooth Criminal*. These two dance steps owe nothing to time nor to gravity and seem to overcome the rules that fix, commonly, human movement. In a pure Hegelian *Aufhebung*, the *moonwalk* creates the perfect illusion of moving forwards and obtaining, as in a nightmare, the opposite result in moving backwards, unwinding – or rewinding – the continuity of time.

Yes, his most famous *moonwalk*[24] breaks the most evident rule of human locomotion. What is its principle? As we said, the dancer creates an illusion in pretending to move forward, but moving in reality backwards. This paradox – the dancer inclining forwards but only succeeding in moving backwards – leads to the illusion of the ground withdrawing under his feet, a kind of invisible moving walkway that swipes the dancer away, in the opposite direction. The success of this dance seems due to a condensation of several experiences at one time: First of all, the *moonwalk* stems on the oneiric experience, potentially filled with anguish, that everybody knows: walking without getting anywhere. Jackson surprises us in showing a movement in reality that we know solely in our dreams.

The somewhat comic effect links the *moonwalk* to the *slapstick* of Charlie Chaplin[25] whom Jackson admired so much that he declared *Smile*, the Chaplin song in *Modern Times*, his favourite song, and visited the widow of Chaplin, Oona O'Neill, in Switzerland to ask her, unsuccessfully, to sell him the *Manoir de Ban* of the *tramp*.

Is the surprise of the *moonwalk* mainly due to the fact that we are confronted with a subversive practice that attacks one of the main laws of locomotion? The *moonwalk* undermines an achievement of humanity: the upright walk and its apparent certainty of moving, of going on. The *moonwalk* draws on the uncanny effect when a perfectly banal habit suddenly becomes emptied of its usual meaning. Jackson draws back whereas trying to move on, and from this apparent contradiction, this paradoxicality, stems the aesthetic pleasure that keeps us watching.

Through his technical virtuosity as a dancer, and mime artist, he produces the illusion of a moving walkway that takes him farther and farther away in the opposite direction of where he initially wanted to go. It is this gap steadily widening between intention and result that gives Jackson's *moonwalk* an even tragic dimension. It shows the irreductible differences between effort, purpose and result – the more he goes on, the more he steps back.

Therefore, the *moonwalk* becomes a metaphor of the postmodern subject that, even while spending enormous amounts of energy to go on, can't help stagnation or even regression. Jackson offers us a sharp critique of the naive notion of progress – his *moonwalk* is enacting a subject capable of rewinding *himself* and thus, to triumph over the inflexible arrow of time. Through his artful inversion of time and space, we witness a subject that unchains himself from chronology and is capable of travelling back in time.

The jubilation that the *moonwalk* triggers in the fascinated public seems to have its roots in the unconscious – to see someone obtaining the opposite of what he was out for may remind us in a non threatening, playful way of our own divisions, shortcomings and contradictions. Being confronted with the opposite of our goals is frequent in our human condition. Primarily frustrating,[26] this experience is transcended by the illusion even reinforced by the illusion of mastering this frustration.

The pleasure principle is restored by such a subversive use of the body. The anguish due to the reality principle and the frustrations it imposes is relieved thanks to beauty and humour.

Whereas Jackson's *moonwalk* plays on the chord of time, he varies another basic fact of human experience: gravity. In his *lean*, the famous dance step he invented for the clip of *Smooth Criminal*, the dancers incline more than 45 degrees forward. Special shoes fixed to the ground by nails prevent them from falling, Jackson having patented this model on 26 October 1993, under the file number 52 55 452. The *lean* seems to be a triumph of defying gravity, the dancers inclining themselves beyond their own centre of gravity, then pulling themselves backward again. But the illusion of their defiance of gravity is only made possible by their shoes firmly held by a sophisticated nail system that clips them to the ground.[27] Both the dancing techniques and the aesthetic programme of MJ exemplifiy his wish to push the limits and, by and by, attest his total intolerance of any boundaries. The same attack of boundary and norm was to be found in the addiction that MJ developed to plastic surgery.

Perspectives of research

At the end of our article, we are far from having finished our exploratory work on Michael Jackson. Several perspectives of research may be drawn here briefly.[28]

How may we explain for example the extraordinary attraction MJ exerted on followers that pay tribute to him all over the world through imitating his *moonwalk* or the famous choreography of *Thriller* that were, for instance, in 2007 performed by the inmates of Cebu Provincial Detention and Rehabilitation Center, a maximum security prison in the Philippines or, in 2013, by the fanfare of the University of Ohio?[29]

Furthermore, we need a sharper analysis of the psychopathology of Michael's fans who deified him and, at his death, collapsed in planetary grief. For instance, the case of a Belgian male nurse, Emmanuel T., who spent all his money to get his face fixed as Michael's may be worth closer scrutiny. How did Emmanuel T. ask for his aesthetic surgery? How did this project and the multiple interventions impact on his identity? What role was played by projection, identification and his own narcissistic void? It may be interesting to investigate the phenomena of impersonators, no artist having inspired so many look-alikes as Michael Jackson, from nameless candidates in, for example, *Britain's got Talent*, to impersonators making their living out of their imitation of MJ. What motivation have Aziz Mezouar (Marocco), Cricri Jackson, Jimmy More (Canada), Mamadou Camara (Afrique de l'Ouest), Michael Gregorio (Arras), Trifun, un fan bulgare, Michael Jam[30] and Navi, the *official impersonator* of Michael Jackson? What brings these impersonators to sacrifice their own self in order to resemble their idol and deny MJ's personal tragedy, the most famous man in the world not knowing who he was? Because Michael Jackson did not like the 'man in the mirror' he saw each morning and he was perhaps the only man on earth not wanting to be Michael Jackson.

From a more sociological point of view, it may be of interest to carry out a systematic study of the websites the fans of Michael Jackson created in the United States, in Great Britain, in France, in Switzerland, in Germany, in Belgium... in order to assure a social cohesion and a strong sense of belonging to a group which is defined by worshipping their idol and by sharing objects or private information on MJ that gain an almost fetishistic value.[31] On youtube.com, it will be promising to analyse the comments the fans leave, as an antic Greek choir, on songs or clips that were created by MJ. The comparisons from the discourse of the fan communities in different countries might offer us the opportunity to learn more about an anthropology of admiration.

Postmodern sociological theories on celebrity culture may be actualised in regard to the Jacksons. We may analyse the official websites of Michael Jackson, of his father Joseph Jackson, his sisters La Toya[32] and Janet Jackson, his brothers

Jermaine, Randy and Tito[33] and, finally, the webside of the *Jackson 5* group.[34] Based on the semiotics of these medias, we may analyse how these websites convey a self-promotional image and contribute to the creation of a 'starisation' and a modern myth of the Jacksons. Narratives of themselves, self-promotion and invention of Michael Jackson may be helpfully compared through the study of the three autobiographies actually available, Michael Jackson's, Katherine's and La Toya's.[35]

Numerous psychaonalysts are interested in the rich symptomatology of Michael Jackson, inviting us to rethink the relationship between genius and madness (Houssier 2013; Givre 2013). Alleged paedophilia, phobias of illness, dysmorphophobia, multiple addictions (compulsive spending, dependency on various pills, drug abuse), heavy insomnia, paranoid episodes, megalomania, Münchhausen syndrome, Peter Pan syndrome, Bambi syndrome, borderline – all these clinical elements should be discussed to throw light on the complex psychic functioning of the star. Particular attention should be paid to the family story and to the sibling complex of Michael Jackson, eighth in a row of ten, born after a twin, Brando, who had died at birth. Did his creativity stem from this tragic event and set the standards for the theme of the ideal double that MJ pursued in his *œuvre* and in his plastic surgery (Schauder 2009)? What degree of liberty did Michael Jackson have to unchain himself from his family where incestuous elements and the American dream of success had fused into an explosive mixture? Finally, what theories did this great artist himself create about his art? In conclusion, much more research has to be done, using multiple viewpoints – i.e. the musciological, sociological, neurological, philosophical and psychoanalytical approaches – to keep up with the fascinating complexity of the 'King of Pop'. *MJ – RIP.*

Notes

1 Cf. the conferences *Regarding Michael Jackson: Performing Racial, Gender, and Sexual Difference.* A two-day conference event at Yale University, 24–25 September 2004. Sponsored by the African American Studies Department and the Larry Kramer Initiative for Lesbian and Gay Studies. Organised by Uri McMillan and Seth Clark Silberman; *Reconstructing the Image of Michael Jackson: Explorations of Body, Spirit, and Society.* Erskine Peters Symposium on Thursday, 25 March 2010. Organised by Dr. Richard Pierce, Chair of the Africana Studies Department in order to explore the legacy of MJ from sociological, anthropological, historical, and literary viewpoints. In France, Sylvie Tordjman organised on 25 June 2010 an international conference *Surdouance, singularité et étrangeté – Le cas de Michael Jackson* at the University of Rennes 1. Her article on Mozart and MJ is currently in press. An interdisciplinary conference project that the author presented in 2010 to the Centre Culturel International de Cerisy was unfortunately not selected for programmation.

2 The author developed this article in the context of several of her works on Michael Jackson (cf. Schauder (2009), Schauder (2011a, b), Schauder (2012a, b), Schauder (2013)).

3 Note that the climax in the song *The Man in the Mirror* is the word 'change'.

4 As if he wants to illustrate the famous Mallarmé verse *On the Tomb of Edgar Poe*: 'Tel qu'en Lui-même enfin l'éternité le change': 'As to Himself eternity changes him at last'.

5 In this sequence, the influence of Christian representations of the human body coming from and returning to dust is all too evident.

6 In *Captain Eo* and in *Scream*, the boundaries between man and machine and between time and space are lifted, also.
7 Cf. Martin Bashir's documentary, *Living with Michael Jackson* (2004), that triggered his second trial for child molestation.
8 Levinas, E. (1995).
9 'Ethics, for Levinas, is what is in me without coming from me. Through myself, I persevere in me being, in my being "inter-ested" or "conatus essendi". Something strange occurs which disturbs this spontaneity, in order to "dis-inter-est" me, cuts me off from myself. This is the figure of the "defection of being", of the face of the other. The "face" of the other intrudes into my being and disturbs my tranquillity, it questions my right to persevere in my being and to use the world as if it were my own. The root of the moral is the "what were you going to do?" which I read on the face of the other.' (Spinoza 1994; author's own translation.) (Thus, in contemplating the devastated face of Michael Jackson, we may only question 'what were you supposed to do to you?')
10 It is a tragedy that this violence missed its original object in producing mere self-destruction facing the horror of an impossible identity. Cf. the parody of the facial changes www.dactari.fr: *mike-morph*.
11 For example, his father made him dance barefooted on a hot plate to teach him to lift his legs rapidly. He would peer through the window with a halloween mask on his face to teach his kids not to sleep with the window open. This archaic fright will play an important role in *Thriller*.
12 Pathetically, the child star had no childhood and tried to win it back through his art and his Peter Pan complex that he materialised in his 2,800-acre (11 km^2) Neverland Valley Ranch near Los Olivos, CA. Cf. the song *Have You Seen my Childhood?* openly melancholic and naive in following the assumption that childhood is paradise lost. Freud would have told him another fairy tale.
13 Cf. his discourse in March 2001 at Cambridge University on the topic of family when, receiving the *doctor honoris causa*, MJ stated that 'for Kermit, it is difficult to be green'.
14 It is notable that Michel Jackson was the first black artist to be played on MTV.
15 The repeated resetting of the nasal septum leaves MJ in the end with a nose completely broken down, forcing him to wear a prosthesis. Eminem in his clip loaded with hatred makes fun out of the misfortune of his former idol.
16 Who, at the death of MJ, expressed his admiration for the artist and had not a word for his lost son.
17 Instead of symbolically killing his father, Michael Jackson, through plastic surgery, killed resemblance, filiation, heritage, likeness, to constitute, finally, a pure strangeness that undid even otherness.
18 It is the classical question of all children, opening their oedipal dynamics and capacity of thought.
19 In Greek tragedy, the hubris is an excess of ambition and pride that ultimately causes the transgressor's ruin who dared to defy the gods.
20 It is commonly acknowledged that Michael Jackson had no real love affair, his two marriages – the first to Lisa Marie Presley, the second to Debbie Rowe – being pure cover-ups.
21 Questioned by the press about the white colour of these two children and insinuating doubts on the reality of his fatherhood, MJ answered: 'Oh, my sperm is white'.
22 MJ states in an interview that the surrogate mother was inseminated with his own sperm.
23 Kenny Ortega, training the dancers for the show *This Is It* explains to them: 'you are all extensions of Michael Jackson'.
24 The appellation is somewhat improper – walking on the moon is, according to the different laws of gravitation, very easy: the astronaut is almost weightless, his steps propulse him up – and forwards. In the contrary, Jackson performs in his *moonwalk* a walk backwards.
25 MJ's *moonwalk* is influenced as well by the mime artist Marcel Marceau and the fascination MJ had for the dance steps of James Brown he imitated as a child. Held instead of his

concerts in 2009, the exposition *Michael Jackson* in the O2 in London showed in a clip the historical influences of MJ's dance: Cab Calloway and the Nicolas Brothers.

26 One may say that the *moonwalk* figures the subject and its symptom, the conflict between desire and defense that intervenes in its formation or in the hysterical attack where torturer and victim share one body.

27 At one concert, you may see a dancer that is not able to undo the clip by moving swiftly aside, thus undoing the magic.

28 An interdisciplinary research project that the author presented in March 2010 to the Agence Nationale de Recherche in France was unfortunately rejected.

29 http://quebec.huffingtonpost.ca/2013/10/22/la-fanfare-de-luniversite-de-lohio-recree-le-moonwalk-de-michael-jackson_n_4143082.html

30 Cf. www.michaeljam.com or casafree.fr, where one might see the best impersonators of MJ.

31 Cf. www.mjfrance.com; www.mjfanclub.net; www.mjackson.fr; mjjplanet.xooit.com; www.jackson.ch; www.mjfc-jam.com; www.malibufanclub.de; www.mjworld.net; www.mjbackstage.be; www.fanpop.com.

32 One is fascinated by the mimicry that LaToya displays, choosing the same aesthetic surgery and bleaching her skin like her famous brother.

33 As far as we know, the two other brothers, Jackie and Marlon, don't have individual websites.

34 Cf. www.jackson5abc.com; www.janetjackson.com; www.jermainejackson-fanclub.com; www.joseph-jackson.de; www.latoyaonline.com; www.michaeljackson.com; www.randyjackson.com; www.titojackson.com.

35 Cf. Jackson (1988); Jackson (1990); Jackson (1992). LaToya Jackson famously chronicled the tumultuous childhood of the Jackson siblings – including charges of physical and sexual abuse by Joseph Jackson, but Janet and others of her siblings disputed LaToya's account (Jackson, David and David 2011; see also http://www.biography.com/people/janet-jackson-9542443?page=1).

References

Anon. (2009) *Michael Jackson: The Official Exhibition.* Exhibition catalogue. London: O2 centre.

Bashir, M. (2004) *Living with Michael Jackson.* London: British Broadcasting Corporation.

Beaune, J.-C. (ed.) (2004) *La Vie et la Mort des Monstres*, Seyssel: Champ Vallon.

Boteach, S. (2009) *The Michael Jackson Tapes: A Tragic Icon Reveals His Soul in Intimate Conversation*, New York: Vanguard Press.

Boudsocq, S. (2004) *Michael Jackson: La Face Cachée d'une Légende.* Saint-Victor-d'Epine: City Editions.

Brown, S. (2005) *Michael Jackson, the Man Behind the Mask,* New York: Select Books.

Cachin, O. (2009) *Michael Jackson Pop Life.* Paris: Alphée Éditions.

Cadman, C. (2003a) *Jacksons Number Ones*, Sandy: Authors On Line Ltd.

Cadman, C. (2003b) *Michael Jackson the Solo Years*, Sandy: Authors On Line Ltd.

Campbell, L.D. (1993) *Michael Jackson: The King of Pop*, Wellesley, MA: Branden Books.

Dalmazzo, A. (2009) 'Charismes, identités, fanatismes. Le charisme médiatique et les fans de Michael Jackson. l'idéal et le monstre'. Doctoral Thesis, Université Paris II.

Dalmazzo, A. (2013) 'Une adolescence incarnée', *Adolescence*, 31(4): 979–993.

Dodd, P. (2008) *Michael Jackson (1958–2009).* London, Gründ: Endeavour.

Fisher, M. (ed., 2009) *The Resistible Demise of Michael Jackson*, Winchester, UK: Zero Books.

Gautier, Y. (2005) *Michael Jackson, de l'Autre Côté du Miroir.* Paris: Publibook.

Givre, P. (2013) 'Fantasmes à vif', *Adolescence*, 31(4): 1005–1030.

Grant, A. (2009) *Michael Jackson: The Visual Documentary, 1958–2009. The Official Tribute Edition*, London: Omnibus Press.

Gray, T. (2009) *Michael Jackson – Before He was King.* USA: Chronicle editions.

Guest, L. (2006) *The Trials of Michael Jackson.* USA: Aureus Publishing.

Henning, S. (2009) *The Book the Media Doesn't Want You to Read.* USA: Author House.

Historisches Museum Speyer (2009) *Idole.* Exhibition catalogue.

Houssier, L. (2013) 'Du lunaire au corps fetichisé', *Adolescence*, 31(4): 995–1004.

Inrockuptibles Hors Série (2009) *Michael Jackson La vraie Historie. Sa Vie, sa Musique, sa Mort* (in press).

Jackson, J., David, A. and David, R. (2011) *True You: A Journey to Finding and Loving Yourself*, South Orange: Gallery Books/Karen Hunter Publishing.

Jackson, K. (1990). *My Family, The Jacksons*, New York: St. Martin's Paperbacks.

Jackson, L. (1992). *LaToya Jackson – Jackson Story* (Re-edited French edition in collaboration with François Jouffa (2009) released with the title *Michael Jackson, La Légende*), Paris: Stock.

Jackson, M. ([1988] 2009) *Moonwalk: An Autobiography* (French translation by F. Hayward), Paris: Michel Lafon.

Jackson, M. ([1992] 2009) *Dancing the Dream: Poems and Reflections*, New York: Doubleday.

Jackson, M. (2006) *My World: The Official Photobook*, vol 1. Hollywood: Triumph International/ MJJ Productions.

Jones, A. (2007) *Michael Jackson: A Conspiracy.* i-Universe, USA: i-Universe.

Jones, J. and Lewis, D. (2005) *Michael Jackson, The King of Pop: An Anthology*, London: Amber Books.

Laurent, S. (2009a) 'Peaux blanches, masques noirs', *Revue Internationale des Livres et des Idées*, 9, January/February.

Laurent, S. (2009b) 'Il était une fois Michael Jackson', 29 June. Online. Available HTTP: <www.laviedesidees.fr>.

Lavigue, L. (2009) *Michael Forever...* Paris: Hugo et Cie.

Levinas, E. (1995) *Altérité et Transcendance*, Montpellier: Fata Morgana, coll.

L'Hermitte, D. (2009a) 'Michael Jackson, la légende', *Paris: Hors Série Noise Magazine.*

L'Hermitte, D. (2009b) *Michael Jackson, L'Ultime Biographie*, Enghien-les-Bains: Editions Premium.

Moix, Y. (2009) *Cinquante Ans dans la Peau de Michael Jackson*, Paris: Grasset.

Runkel, P. and Krämer, R. (2009) *Remember the Time: Erinnerungen an den King of Pop*, Germany: Lingen.

Schauder, S. (2009) *Fabrique du Corps et Fiction de Soi à l'Adolescence: Notes sur Michael Jackson (1958–2009)*, Communication at the Journées de la SFPE-AT, CMME, Sainte Anne, Paris, 28–29 November.

Schauder, S. (2011a) *Notes Sur le Clip 'Thriller' (1983)*, Communication at the Fifth Colloque Babylone (Art, Littérature et Psychanalyse), IMM, Paris, 25 March, 2011.

Schauder, S. (2011b) *The Multiple Bodies of Michael Jackson: A Paradigm to Understand Contemporary Adolescent Disorders?* Communication at the International Conference on Body Image and Identity in Contemporary Society, CUNY, New York, 8–10 April, 2011.

Schauder, S. (2012a) *Michael Jackson ou la Métamorphose Négative de l'Adolescence*; *Hysterically Yours – Michael Jackson: The Other Side of His Art*, Communication at the Body and Art Conference (The Image of Hysteria in the 21st Century), Vienna, 22 November 2012.

Schauder, S. (2012b) 'Michael Jackson ou la métamorphose négative de l'adolescence', *L'Autre, Cliniques, Cultures et Sociétés*, 1(37): 108–114.

Schauder, S. (2013) 'Michael Jackson's *Thriller* video: a negative metamorphosis of the hero in adolescence ?', *Adolescence*, 31(4): 965–977.

Spinoza, B. de ([1677] 1994) *Ethique*, Paris: Folio.

Taraborrelli, J.R. (1988/ 1991/ 2004) *Michael Jackson: The Magic and the Madness*, New York: Headline and Pan Books.

Discography and filmography of Michael Jackson and *The Jackson Five*

Albums of The Jackson Five

Diana Ross Presents The Jackson 5 (1969)
ABC (1970)
Third Album (1970)
The Jackson 5 Christmas Album (1970)
Maybe Tomorrow (1971)
Goin' Back To Indiana (1971)
Lookin' Through The Windows (1972)
Skywriter (1973)
In Japan! (1973)
Get It Together (1973)
Dancing Machine (1974)
Moving Violation (1975)
Joyful Jukebox Music (1976)
Boogie (1979)

Albums of The Jacksons

The Jacksons (1976)
Goin' Places (1977)
Destiny (1978)
Triumph (1980)
Live (1981)
Victory (1984)
2300 Jackson Street (1989)

Compilations

Greatest Hits (1971)
Anthology (1976)
Soulsation! (1995)
Jackson 5: The Ultimate Collection (1995)
The Essential Jacksons (2004) (US version)
The Very Best of The Jacksons (2004) (international version)
I Want You Back! Unreleased Masters (2009)

Solo albums under the label Motown

Got to Be There (1972)
Ben (1972)
Music and Me (1973)
Forever, Michael (1975)

Solo albums under the label Sony

Off the Wall (1979)
Thriller (1982)
Bad (1987)
Dangerous (1991)
HIStory – Past, Present, and Future: Book 1 (1995)
Invincible (2001)

Compilations under the labels Motown and Sony

One Day in Your Life (1981)
Farewell My Summer Love (1984)
Blood on the Dance Floor – HIStory in the Mix (1997)
Greatest Hits – HIStory Volume I (2001)
Number Ones (2003)
The Ultimate Collection (2004)
The Essential Michael Jackson (2005)
Thriller 25 (2008)
King of Pop (2008)
The Collection (2009)
This Is It (2009)
The Remix Suite (2009)

DVD with the clips or concerts

Michael Jackson (1992) *Life in Bucarest: The Dangerous Tour.*
Michael Jackson (2009) *Dangerous: The Short Films.*
Michael Jackson (2001) *Video Greatets Hits. HIStory*. MVX.
Michael Jackson History. The King of Pop 1958–2009 (2009). ITN Source. Exclusive Moving Footage.
The Life and Death of Michael Jackson 1958–2009 Memoria.

Filmography

Year	Character	Role
1978	*The Wiz*	The Scarecrow
1986	*Captain EO*	Captain EO
1988	*Moonwalker*	Himself
1990	*Listen Up*	Himself
1991	*The Simpsons*	Leon Kompowsky
1996	*Ghosts*	The Maestro and the Mayor of the City
2002	*Men in Black II*	Agent M
2004	*Miss Cast Away*	Agent MJ
2009	*This Is It*	Himself

Documentaires

1983: *The Making of Michael Jackson's Thriller,* presented by John Landis
1993: *Oprah Winfrey Interviews Michael Jackson*
2003: *The One,* presented by Ann Rim
2003: *Living with Michael Jackson,* presented by Martin Bashir.
2003: *Michael Jackson's Private Home Movies*
2004: *Michael Jackson: du Rêve à la Réalité,* presented by Allan Moyle
2005: *Michael Jackson's Secret Childhood*
2005: *Michael Jackson's Boys*
2007: *Michael Jackson en Quête de Vérité,* presented by Jacques Peretti
2009: *Dr. Prince and Mr. Jackson,* presented by Philips Priestley
2009: *This Is It,* film documentary presented par Kenny Ortega

Docu-fiction

Griffith, J. (2003) *Michael Jackson, Man in the Mirror: Une Star dans l'Ombre.* Champigny sur Marne: Emylia DVD Production.

Television

The Jackson Five (The Jackson 5ive) and *The New Jackson 5ive Show* is a television series of American animation in 40 episodes of 22 minutes, created by Jules Bass and Arthur Rankin Jr. It was broadcast between 11 September 1971 and 11 September 1973 on ABC.

11

FROM CATHARSIS TO THE CATHARTIC

Toward a post-dramatic theory of representation

Renata Mattos-Avril and Jean-Michel Vives

The theatrical forms which emerged during the twentieth century and qualified as post-dramatic (Lehmann 2002) aspired to be essentially and resolutely non-Aristotelian: the quest for the catharsis as defined by Aristotle was no longer their aim. Briefly, we can recall how Aristotle presents the theatrical catharsis in his *Poetics*:

> And, by representing the pity and the fright, it (the representation) attains a purification (catharsis) of this kind of emotion.
>
> *(Aristotle 1980: 53)*

This 'explanatory' sentence consecrated by Aristotle to the notion of catharsis in his *Poetics* presents an enigma that has not ceased to fascinate those who have been trying to analyse the effects of tragedy. The term, borrowed from the medical vocabulary – 'purification, purgation' – seems to be employed there in a metaphorical way without this being stated clearly. The text of the *Poetics* is only explicit about the experiences linked to catharsis: the pity and the fear as affects, emotive troubles (*pathèmata*), always presented as painful in the different chapters where they are in question. The catharsis lies in this paradoxical and mysterious faculty, which would be specific to the tragic spectacle, of transforming unpleasant feelings in pleasure. We could repeat here the words from Lacan, borrowed from Molière, who wanted to make fun of the Freudian solution of the sublimation:

> Will we be satisfied to say…that, indeed, the aim has changed, that it was sexual and that it is no longer? …From what it should be concluded that the sexual libido has become desexualized. And that is the reason why your daughter is dumb!
>
> *(Lacan 1959/1986: 133)*

This enigmatical cathartic alchemy has been a constant battlefield for the commentators since the Renaissance, after the interest in the text of Aristotle resumed, and until our days.

The classical interpretation, offered by humanists as well as by many theoreticians of Classicism, makes the cathartic process a properly moral resort: by being shown the grievous result of 'bad' passion, the tragic spectacle would purge – or cure – the spectator from these same passions (whatever they are and not only simply the terror and the pity). Dubitative, Corneille (1987: 145) wonders, not without humour, what would be the passions from which *Oedipus the King* could really purge us: from incest and parricide[1]? In spite of these questions and critiques, the Aristotelian model and its various interpretations remained the one that radically guided the theatrical thought until the beginning of the twentieth century.

Whereas all theatrical aesthetics until the middle of the twentieth century, for over 2500 years of dramatic productions, were measured against the Aristotelian proposition (Florence 2006: 39–46), according to which all representation should convene the dimension of illusion, authorising the identification of the spectator with the hero and producing catharsis by the experimentation of fear and pity, post-dramatic theatre would claim to have broken with this tradition. The knell sounds for dramatic texts built on a plot and recognizable characters. The text, which was during a long time the site of the catharsis, is forsaken for the benefit of the stage and its powers. Powers that, we must remember, were undervalued, even refused by Aristotle in the production of the cathartic effect. Thus, Aristotle affirms in Chapter 14 of his *Poetics*:

> The fright and the pity can certainly be born from the spectacle, but they can also be born from the system of the facts itself: this is the process that holds the first rank and that reveals the best poet. It is indeed necessary that, independently of the spectacle, the story could be therefore constructed by acquiring the facts produced there and that we could shiver and be taken by pity in the presence of what is happening: that is what we would feel by listening to the story of Oedipus. To produce this effect by the means of the spectacle scarcely reveals the art: it is a matter of the staging, of the '*mise en scène*'. Those who produce by the means of the spectacle not the frightening but only the monstrous, do not have anything to do with the tragedy; for it is not any pleasure which is required by tragedy but the pleasure itself. However, as the pleasure that the poet must produce comes from the pity and from the fright roused by the representative activity, it is obvious that he must register it in the facts while composing.
>
> *(Aristotle 1980: 81)*

The text of Aristotle reveals here an opposition that will guide our thought: it concerns the opposition between seeing and listening. According to Aristotle, the cathartic dynamics must be caused by what the audience hears and not by what it sees; the spectacle could belong to it without having the most important part. This opposition between vision and hearing, and even more particularly the emphasis on the latter, interests the psychoanalyst precisely in what the procedure invented by Freud sets up: the dismissal of the gaze for the benefit of listening.

The departure from hypnosis, previously utilised by Freud, effectively means the departure from the importance of the gaze. We can evoke the spectacles that were the (re)presentations of hysterical patients organised by Charcot in the Salpêtrière hospital (Didi-Huberman 1982) in which the question of 'making see' was essential; yet ultimately, hypnosis was deposed as a preferred method, giving place instead to an emerging technique based on a human voice delivering a narrative. To Freud, interested in the construction of the psychoanalytical practice, as to Aristotle is his commitment to determine the conditions to the surfacing of the properly tragic emotion, the cathartic issues will be only identified in a correctly articulated narrative and not in an outburst of affects delivered through images to the avid sight of the spectator.

The mention of the spectacle as a possible source of the tragic emotion, which Aristotle makes in Chapter XIV of his *Poetics*, can act indeed only as a foil and allows us to define more precisely how the tragic emotion can be revealed *in fine* being the result of the arrangement of facts according to a specific order.

In this case, two feelings that are, according to Aristotle, the only ones entirely pertinent to the art of tragedy, namely fright and pity, are elicited not through vision but through hearing. Audience members presented with a tragedy are asked to exercise their faculties as spectators far more than as listeners. It is by mediation of speech ('by apprehending the facts which are being produced', 'by listening to the story of Oedipus') that catharsis can be successfully carried out.

The visual, spectacular dimension of the tragedy is secondary, and even if it can contribute to the production of the tragic effect, its principle remains external to the art – an innate weakness that Aristotle was unable to support. Moreover, the spectacle tends to require forms that are totally external to the tragic, such as the monstrous. The monstrous provokes a fright in a rough state, an immediate fright, a physical trouble situated more on the side of terror than of fright and not allowing for any reflection.

Aristotle says that it is simple to provoke this kind of troubled state in the spectator by presenting him or her with horrible visions and he also affirms that, by privileging the visual spectacle, the poet is complicit in this easy solution. The 'Grand-Guignol', popular in France from the late nineteenth to the early twentieth centuries, which was built essentially around showing terrifying images, demonstrates sufficiently that a theatre of the monstrous on the stage does not have much in common with the art of tragedy.

On this subject, one of the oeuvres consecrated to the history of the Grand-Guignol starts with the following sentence:

> The Grand-Guignol ..., which, from 1896 until 1962, was installed in the Cité Chaptal in Paris and proposed more than three hundred plays, was born from images.
>
> *(Pierron 2002: 8)*

The Aristotelian thesis is that once we give privilege to this visual dimension, to the detriment of poetic work of constructing the form and the 'purgation' of the emotions, tragedy no longer exists: what is left is the monstrous. By abandoning listening in favor of a visual representation, we leave the field of art and of aesthetic delight (*jouissance*) to enter into another dimension that we will endeavor to address later on.

Yet, the post-dramatic theatre proposes a shift, or an off-centring, that seems to locate the dimension spe(cta)cular in the centre of its process. This off-centring can be found in the transition from textocentrism to privileging the stage (Naugrette 2011: 173). The director, 'the poet of the stage', becomes more important than the author/playwright, the poet of words. In post-dramatic theatre, the plot is often secondary to the scenic writing; it is the director who uses the visual effects, sometimes provocative or shocking, to explore what is there 'to look at'.

If, etymologically, theatre is the place where we go in order to see, this issue has never been as poignant as in the last few decades. The effects were violently felt during the Avignon Festival in 2005, the edition precisely dedicated to the 'poets of the stage', as announced in the program. There were strong reactions to the performance of the troupe of Jan Fabre about *The History of Tears* (*L'Histoire des Larmes*) at the opening of the 59th festival, which was often met with incomprehension and sometimes even rejection by spectators as well as critics and artists (Banu and Bruno 2005). In a performance like this, the dimensions of the body and of the sensoriality offer less of an aesthetic of re-presentation than of re-presence.

The Aristotelian propositions that guided the theatrical compass are no longer at the heart of theatrical enterprise. Thus, the text concerns more and more a fragmentary writing, slices of texts freely arranged. Theatre is made out of the play, privileging the stage where the creators of theater exhibit pieces of 'the prose of the world'. Prose that makes less to listen than it gives to see. The post-dramatic theatre proposes less a dramatic writing than a scenic writing.

Shall we conclude from this that the catharsis must be put away on the shelf of cast-off accessories? That is not certain, for while the catharsis – seeking fright and pity in a representation (*mimesis*) in the Aristotelian sense – is held at bay, the cathartic – as the excess of the work of the representation – is made omnipresent. If catharsis – as a witness of the identification to the character and to the construction of the plot – is disappearing, the cathartic – which we can circumscribe following C. Naugrette (2011) as what exceeds, in all the senses of the term, the representation and consequently the identification and its support, the body – invades the dramatic text, theatrical representation and critical discourse.

We can locate in post-dramatic production the search for an effect – the cathartic effect – and not of an identification that magically would carry the public into a vast fusion of affects. By seeking the contrary of such a fusion of consciences (in the sense of the classical aims of the dramatic theatre, originated from liturgies, ceremonial rites and sacrifices), by seeking to disillusion through the exercise of a cynical irony, what is refused is the induction (cathartic, mimetic) of pity and compassion. This requires that the actors would be endangered, exposed in their flesh beyond the conventional exercises and exigencies of the profession, in a direct body proximity, without the protecting fabric of the play, of the 'as if'... On the other hand, the public can be overturned, displaced, destabilized... sometimes pushed to the limits of the bearable.

Finally, the text can come from any source: it is subject to editing, to collage... to discontinuity. Time can either be stretched ad infinitum or accelerated. The traditional law of the three unities (place, time, action), which was the guiding principle of a psychological theatre, of a theatre of the self and of identification, is no longer in use.

Nowadays, the practices of rupture, reduction of images; sensorial demands; implosion of the narrative; and disintegration of character up to the point of obliteration of any character identified as 'self', propose a new challenge concerning not only the link between stage and theatre, spectator and actor, dramatic author and director, text and staging but also between affect and representation. This questioning eventually starts affecting the notion of identification: identity is not only shifting but sometimes impossible.

The contemporary stage does not aim at the production of particular identifications; it is a theatre of the present and of performance. The contemporary theatre wants to show the real, at the edge of two realms: one of the most absolute concreteness (the physical body, sometimes reduced to flesh, to bodily wastes...) and the most carefully constructed abstraction, staging, *mise en scène*. The contemporary stage proposes a new grammar of the body and identities that obliges us to rethink, in the light of its experimentations, what a body is and an identity is in a post-dramatic era. We propose that these new modalities of being and/or having a body, of manufacturing or not manufacturing identity, which are produced by contemporary representation, may be named cathartic.

While catharsis was essentially related to listening – Freud, besides, in his text *Psychopathic Characters in the Stage*, brings it closer to the effect produced by a witty remark (Freud 1905/2006: 319), the cathartic of the contemporary theatre would favor a plural sensorial dimension by associating voice and glance in a process that leads to fracture.

However, the very dimensions of excess and flow lead us to the most current definition of catharsis, allowing us to pinpoint more precisely the cathartic found in the contemporary theatre. In fact, the banal conception of the beneficial effects of a therapeutic action is that the played, authorised expression, free from thoughts (memories...) associated with the liberation of affects (inhibited, uptight, retained...) can only bring a relief, a relaxation of the tensions until then held and, as they were unexpressed, deleterious.

Freud and Breuer elaborated from this conception the method that they precisely chose to name as cathartic. These two authors refer less at this time to the Aristotle of *Poetics* than to the one of *Politics*. Aristotle, indeed, enlightens in his *Politics* how there are individuals possessed

> which will calm themselves under the effect of sacred melodies each time that they have recourse to the melodies which throw the soul out of itself as if they had found there remedy and purging.[2]

The catharsis described by Aristotle in *Politics* is much more direct than the one provoked by tragedy. It does not pass through representation, fable and identification with the character but it operates by acting on the sensibility, on the sensorial level.

There, where theatrical catharsis would be mediated by language, musical catharsis would be immediate, in other words, it would try to avoid mediation of language.

This unmediated modality of catharsis that post-dramatic theatre solicits would permit the spectator to live an experience sometimes in the limit of the supportable. However, its intent would be to make the spectators experience moments of de-signation there where Aristotelian theatre privileged designation. The question of the discursive dimension is present there by the question of staging, of the *mise en scène*. Besides, the musical or poetic schema, more than the dramatic, is present in contemporary theatre, for instance, under the form of repetition, as we already find in Beckett.

This regime of the cathartic is the one from which, it seems, Lacan approaches in the last sessions of his seminary of *The Ethics of Psychoanalysis* to the investigation of Sophocles's *Antigone*, where he gives his analysis of catharsis. Even if this analysis is based on a text that obeys the rules of the *Poetics* of Aristotle, we can point out how it overflows this system, allowing us to apprehend the effects of contemporary representation. According to Lacan, the catharsis is at least as much a matter of affects than of images. We can find there the central place given by post-dramatic theatre to the scopic dimension. However, it's essential to observe here that it concerns an image of a very particular quality and that it has nothing to do with those that surround us in our daily life. Thus, Lacan announces:

> Antigone makes us see in fact the aiming point that defines desire. This aiming goes towards an image that retains I do not know which mystery until now not yet articulable, since it makes the eyes blink at the time we look at it. This image is, though, in the center of the tragedy, since it is the fascinating Antigone herself, it is what fascinates us in its unbearable enthrallment, in what it has of baffling – this victim is terribly voluntary.
>
> It is on the side of this lure that we must seek the true sense, the true mystery, the true scope of the tragedy – on the side of this commotion that it comprises, on the side of the passions, undoubtedly, but of particular passions which are fright and pity, as by their intermediary, by the intermediary of fright and pity, we are purged, purified from everything of this genre. This command, we can gilt and already recognize – this is strictly speaking the series of the imaginary. And we are purged from it by the intermediary of an image.
>
> *(Lacan 1959/1986: 290)*

Catharsis would be considered also as a purgation of the imaginary (in other words, everything that could offer a completeness to man: me – *moi* –, identification to signs from which it tries to apprehend and understand itself) through an image. But through a very particular image. A blinding image, indicates Lacan. Not a filling and reassuring image, but an image that signs beyond the representation.

How should we understand that? The image creates a barrier but also signs towards this other Thing that is beyond any sense, any discourse (Regnault 1997: 81–94; 2011: 239–254). It is an image that, at the same instant, signs beyond representation and veils it. By demolishing the materials of identification, articulated narratives, the unity of time, place and action, post-dramatic theatre allows the emergence of this Other dimension that the work of the representation aims to dissimulate. It is there that we find the cathartic of the post-dramatic theatre, which can be recognised in the thought of Lacan:

> the sense of purification of desire. This purification can only be accomplished, as it is clear when we simply read the statement of Aristotle, if we have at least located the possibility to cross our limits, which are fright and pity.
>
> That is why the tragic *épos* warns the spectator of where is the pole of desire; it shows that access to desire needs to get over not only any fright but also any pity, that the voice of the hero does not tremble in front of anything, and in particular in front of the good of the other. That is why all this is proven in the temporal course of the story, that the subject knows a little bit more than before about the deepest [parts] of himself.
>
> It takes as long as it takes, if we go to French Theatre or to the Theatre of Athens. But finally, if the formulas of Aristotle mean something, that is it. We know what it takes to advance in a certain direction and, my God, if we do not go there, we know why. We can even sense that if we are not exactly clear with the accounts of the desire, that is because we could not have done better. For this is not a route where we can advance without paying anything.
>
> The spectator is undeceived on this, that even for those who advance to the extreme of his/her desire, everything is not that easy. But he/she is also undeceived – and that is the essential – on the value of the prudence to which he/she is opposed, on the completely relative value of his/her beneficial reasons, on the attachments, on the pathological interests (…) that can retain him/her on this risky route.
>
> *(Lacan 1959/1986: 372)*

The catharsis – in the contemporary form of the cathartic – stills interests thus the contemporary theatrical representation: chase out the Aristotelian catharsis by the gate, it will return by the window in the form of the cathartic. Cathartic that we can henceforth interpret as come out from the purging of fright and pity, which are passions that retain the subject in his path towards desire. The illusion of finding consistency by means of the object and even of narrative – strongly called into question by the post-dramatic creation – would find its counterpart in the excess linked to representation, which would not be interpreted as excessiveness but as a deep challenge of the work of representation.

Post-dramatic theatre would thus have the function of reminding us which overpass of the limit supposes the experience of our desire. It would allow us to feel, to approach, to play with this limit.

In sum, the contemporary cathartic would permit the subject to sense the Thing behind the object, to reveal and to veil at the same time this absolute and forever lost object of desire as well as to take the risk of exposing him/herself there. The contemporary cathartic would also find the very ancient function that Aristotle assigned to theatrical catharsis: 'awake the human sense' (Aristotle 1980: 99), for it would interrogate this mythic instant when I burst out as a subject in the moment that I separated myself from this first object.

Post-dramatic theatre would become thus this place where the intrapsychic forces that work in every human would be incarnated and played in an immediate way. It would allow us to experience, in the paradoxical moment of a representation often aiming to denounce itself as space of illusion, our human and unconscious condition: condemned to the work of representation (Aulagnier 1975), which we hate, for it is the witness of our impossible completeness.

Notes

1 'Although I cannot see which passion it gives us to purge neither of what we could correct ourselves on its example'.
2 Aristotle, *Politique,* Chapter 7, 1342a, 7–11.

References

Aristotle (1980) *La Poétique*, text, translation and notes by Roselyne Dupont-Roc and Jean Lallot, Paris: Seuil.
Aristotle (1960) *Politique*, Chapter 7, Paris: Les Belles Lettres, 1342a 7–11.
Aulagnier, P. (1975) *La Violence de l'Interprétation*, Paris: P.U.F.
Banu, G. and Bruno, B. (eds) (2005) *Le Cas Avignon 2005. Regards Critiques*, Paris: L'Entretemps.
Corneille, P. ([1660] 1987) 'Discours de la tragédie et des moyens de la traiter selon le vraisemblable ou le nécessaire', 'Trois Discours sur le Poème dramatique' in *Œuvres Complètes*, Tome III, Paris: NRF, Bibliothèque de La Pléiade.
Didi-Huberman, G. (1982) *Invention de l'Hystérie. Charcot et l'Iconographie Photographique de la Salpetrière*, Paris: Macula.
Florence, J. (2006) 'Poétique théâtrale et esthétique freudienne', *Insistance*, 2, Toulouse: Eres.
Freud, S. ([1905] 2006) 'Personnages psychopathiques à la scène', in *Œuvres Complètes*, French translation, Paris: P.U.F.
Lacan, J. ([1959] 1986) *Le Séminaire, Livre VII, L'Ethique de la Psychanalyse*, Paris: Seuil.
Lehmann, H.-T. (2002) *Le Théâtre Postdramatrique*, French translation, Paris: L'Arche.
Naugrette, C. (2011) 'Du cathartique dans le théâtre contemporain', in J.-C. Darmon (ed.) *Littérature et Thérapeutique des Passions. La Catharsis en Question*, Paris: Hermann, p. 167–180.

Pierron, A. (2002) *Les Nuits Blanches du Grand-Guignol*, Paris: Seuil.
Regnault, F. (1997) 'Katharsis', in *Conférences d'Esthétique Lacanienne*, Paris: Seuil.
Regnault, F. (2011) 'La catharsis selon Lacan', in *Littérature et Thérapeutique des Passions. La Catharsis en Question*, Paris: Hermann.

12

MODIFIED IMAGES OF THE BODY

New forms of identity with a note on the cadavers of Gunther Von Hagens

Céline Masson

Body/image

Art reflects socio-cultural developments. Our times are awash with intense feelings and extreme images: we are drawn to experiences of excess that challenge our moral standards and elicit strong emotions. Artists subvert the prohibitions of our moral systems: by glorifying violence, exhibiting the body, its parts and waste matter, and even by turning the corpse into an aesthetic object. There are no longer any limits and the very idea of their absence commands a premium of aesthetic pleasure. As the art critic Paul Ardenne writes, 'What is at stake in looking at the extreme is the construction of the self … however, contemporary culture magnifies this feeling, exploits it and constantly tries to push it further' (Ardenne 2006).

Bodies are sometimes mutilated and modified by accidents; these deformations can sometimes make them monstrous. The rapid progress of today's medicine, including virtual medicine that no longer involves the singular physical encounter between the physician and the patient, constantly pushes the body's limits and allows the artist to invent new ways of pursuing creative work in society. However, the body is also glorified because it disappears as a body of flesh. Professor Didier Sicard, the author of 'Medicine Without Body' [La Médecine sans le Corps, 2002] argues:

> The tendency to compartmentalize the body is spreading rapidly, so that in the end medicine is no longer interested in the body itself, apart from the odd traumatic wound or skin eruption. Today's students are hardly ever taught medical semiology, i.e. the study of symptoms and signs, and when they are, it is only as a substitute for the history of medicine and not for its own medical interest. Listening to a patient and watching over his complaint

> is considered a waste of time. An old medical saying tells us: 'Listen to the patient and he will give you the diagnosis'; however, this essential moment is now vanishing.
>
> *(Sicard 2005: 38)*

His following argument seems important to me with respect to the problem of the body/image:

> To examine a patient completely, that is to say, to restore his lost unity to him, is seen as a useless procedure, or even as something indiscreet and bothersome. The sign has been replaced by the image, which sometimes results in grotesque situations, such as when the physician is wondering about an anomalous mammogram, which only represents a small breast abscess, as he could have easily found out, had he simply looked at the breast with his naked eye and not only through the machine...
>
> *(Sicard 2005: 38)*

The image has replaced the sign. The image becomes the body at the expense of the flesh. The body is now an image and any medical appointment can prompt the use of medical imaging techniques while quite often pathology could be identified simply by touching and looking. Imaging now completes the medical gesture.

To put this in other words, today's medicine perceives the body as a set of separate parts; you must go straight to the organ when it lets itself be heard. Virtual images (ultrasound, CT, MRI scans) of organs give us a new body, which is now the site of images and hence dominated by the gaze, at the expense of the physician's hand that used to touch and feel and by doing so established contact with the patient as an entire person, rather than a set of isolated parts. Sicard continues:

> The growing technological transference of the body creates a constant need for refining the equipment. The paradox lies in the growing autonomy of the image vis-à-vis the ever-more-absent body: the image claims its own status and makes its own demands, which are ultimately quite indifferent to its initial justification. In other words, the improvement of the image has to do with maximising its use, not with what it shows.
>
> *(Sicard 2005: 38)*

The French philosopher and historian Bernard Andrieu believes that modifying one's body constitutes a proof of one's freedom, thus conferring on it a historical and social dimension. He continues:

> This maximal historicity of the human body tends to corroborate the social fantasy of a science of personal identity, whereby all natural qualities can be remodeled in man's image. Nature no longer shapes the human body. It is

> now the individual who defines himself through science and who creates his own definition of the natural norm.
>
> *(Andrieu 1994: 21)*

In other words, we create our bodies according to our fantasies, pushing the limits of what is possible ever further. Science lends itself to this creation remarkably well, but the newly promised body comes at a high price, both financial and psychical (it is a body promised by the injunctions of the Superego: be beautiful, young, wrinkle-free, fat-free, etc.). We cannot always obtain the body of our fantasy without suffering the consequences (and neither is it very easy to obtain because a fantasy always necessarily fails to come true, and only because it fails it can continue to fuel desire). The body of one's dreams is a body 'without' the body, without flesh and its many forms, but 'with' certain prostheses that help it 'be' beautiful. The subject creates his own identity with the help of science as the guarantor of the 'natural norm.'

Bodies are equally glorified in the fashion market and in the cosmetics and wellness industry; however, these are adolescent bodies prematurely forced into adulthood, which should then last at least until the age of fifty, the critical point beyond which one should no longer age. This body is a body/image, retouched by software and modified by various devices. However, at the same time, the body has indeed disappeared from the physician's consulting room. Doctors no longer examine it: what is considered important lies inside and can only be accessed using various methods of medical imaging. As if the outer layer, the flesh, the object of touch, no longer held any interest. This is also evidenced by the popularity of cremation, as a way of not having to face the decay of the corpse, which previous generations found so fascinating. The body is ephemeral: it must either go up in smoke or be preserved intact. This leads us to the question of embalming and of today's new forms of preserving the body: plasticine and the conception of the aestheticised corpse (or is it still a corpse?) as seen in the works of the German anatomist and artist Gunther Von Hagens.

This controversial procedure and its goals – aestheticising the body for what are supposedly pedagogical, yet, I would argue, primarily commercial purposes – shows us that bodies have a life after death and, more importantly, that this life can be transformed into cash. Using Von Hagens's work as an example of making art with dead bodies, I would like to discuss, on the border of medicine and contemporary art, how the body becomes inscribed in an economic and political logic that commands a specific form of its treatment.

Von Hagens: a body for eternity

Von Hagens is a medical anatomist whose work combines art with medical pathology; he obtains the material for his 'figural' installations by searching through mortuaries. He uses entire bodies, thus adopting an ambiguous position on the border between art and science; he describes his work as both medical and aesthetic. In the late 1970s, he invented plastination:

> The method consists of extracting, under a vacuum, water and fat from the tissues, and replacing them with silicone rubber or epoxy resin. Entire bodies or organs can thus retain their plasticity; they do not smell and can be preserved for eternity. The principle is simple, but the procedure is more complicated and requires 1000 hours of labour for the entire body. With its skin removed, the body literally becomes a 'skinned corpse.' It is shown in its entire muscular, venous and arterial, and even visceral complexity.
>
> (Le Nouvel Observateur, *18 October, 2001)*

Plastination radically transforms the original human remains, ultimately depriving them of more than 70 per cent of their biological properties. I therefore suggest that we should describe these figures as aestheticised dead bodies, rather than simply corpses because the process of decay has been interrupted for aesthetic purposes.

Von Hagen's scientific procedure is primarily a method of embalming. However, he chooses to exhibit his plastinated bodies in artistic spaces, positioning them according to conventions that are different from those of traditional medical anatomists. The aesthetic effect is produced by creating a certain *mise-en-scène*, which arranges the plastinates in what we could call social poses.

These figures are simultaneously grotesque and repulsive. They can be shown swimming or playing chess; one skinned figure is holding its skin at arm's length. Inspired by Rembrandt, Von Hagens believes that plastination can give life to the fascinating idea of a symbiosis between art and anatomy. It stops decomposition and desiccation so perfectly that human anatomy preserves its intrinsic aesthetics. The artistic, ethical and legal dimensions of his work have been subject to great controversy. France has banned similar kinds of expositions; however, they have attracted six million viewers globally, including two and a half million in Japan and in Germany. The reception of these works raises many questions, including the reasons of those who decide to donate their body. Plastination interrupts the process of decomposition, freezing the body in time and halting the work of death. The dead body, which the scientific procedure transforms into a work of art, is no longer a rotting corpse and therefore ceases to be impure and contagious. After this treatment, once it has been purified, it can be exposed. Plastination makes the dead body visible and aesthetic; it is pleasant to look at and provokes curiosity. Von Hagens's technique can be seen as a modern form of what Roger Caillois has called 'a desacralization ritual (…), which makes a pure or impure person or object part of the profane world' (Caillois 1950: 28–29). The exhibition of these transformed bodies is not a display of death: the plastinated corpses do not represent the effects of death on the body, but result from the scientific work of the living. Looking at them means looking at what is alive and at work. The question lies in the diabolical partnership between art and science.

An article published in *Le Monde* in 2004 reports:

> Gunther von Hagens has three workshops. One is based in Heidelberg, Germany, but the other two have been outsourced to Bishkek in Kyrgyzstan

> and Dalian in China. As a good student of globalization, the workshop owner has made a swift calculation: both Kyrgyzstan and China have skilled workforce, reasonable wages, benevolent legislation and abundant raw materials.
>
> This last element is nonetheless somewhat particular: we are speaking about human bodies. The medical anatomist and aspiring artist Gunther von Hagens has invented a method of preserving corpses called 'plastination.' The procedure consists of a kind of lamination of dead bodies, which then enables all kinds of manipulation, of cutting and coloring, and also of skinning and arranging the bodies in various collective poses. Since 1997, the anatomist has been parading his 'plastinated' bodies around the world, organising spectacular and morbid expositions under the label of 'Körperwelten' ('Body Worlds'). His works have already been seen by almost 14 million visitors throughout the world. A new spectacle, with the financial support of the State of Hesse, has just opened in Frankfurt.
>
> *(Marion 2004)*

In an essay called 'Death or the Dead?' the French historian and anthropologist Jean-Pierre Vernant writes that whenever the dead are subject to a particular treatment, it is a sign that we are dealing with humans. 'The dead are beings who have lost all identity, all form – if a corpse is abandoned, it no longer has a face; the dead person no longer has a memory (...)' (Vernant 2001: 7). We could object to this notion of identity that dead bodies do indeed have an identity, which modern methods help us reveal. In addition, their memory is sustained by the living. However, Vernant emphasises the formlessness of the dead body, its disturbing shapelessness. It seems to me that to some extent, Von Hagen's method and the attraction that plastination holds for its candidates must be understood as effects of the apprehension and anxiety connected to bodily decomposition and the absence of form, leading some individuals to opt for this 'good' form of death. 'Good' for a sorcerer's apprentice; good for those who reject death and find unexpected hope in this method. 'Each society must confront the radical otherness, the extreme absence of form, the non-being par excellence represented by the phenomenon of death' (Vernant 2001: 9). Different cultures and religions have established strategies, conveyed by faith, of conjuring the anxiety we feel about our own body, as well as the bodies of our loved ones, losing their form. Hence the importance of rituals, for example of the Jewish mourning ritual of shiva: for seven days, close relatives gather together to remember the deceased, in order not to be alone, but surrounded by others.

By giving form to death, plastination confers upon the deceased a twenty-first-century version of sainthood; it transforms him or her into a functioning and unchangeable living being, even an immortal one. This is evidenced by the numerous allusions to divine perfection filling the guestbooks of Von Hagen's shows in North America, as well as his own remark that 'the longevity of [his] pieces will exceed that of the mummies of the pharaohs' (National Public Radio 2001: 11).

I therefore argue that the dead person is here turned into a trophy, into a kind of cold icon without transcendence, trapped in the plastic material. The body is 'frozen;' it has no future. In fact, it seems to me that when looking at Von Hagens's figures, we no longer 'see' the dead person or his or her corpse. Regardless of whether it is cremated, buried or embalmed, the dead body is diverted away from death. Death no longer resembles itself. The process is a transgressive act of turning away from death, in order to make corpses resemble living bodies happily going on with their daily activities.

I therefore believe that we must make a distinction between corpses and these plastinated specimens, which precisely seem to be saying 'Anything but death!' in a rejection of the process of physical disappearance. In this sense, they are no longer corpses. They exist in a permanent state of the living dead, like a frozen image deceiving death. And we rejoice at the sight of this masquerade. The difference between the disappearing corpse and the plastinated body is movement. Dead bodies are inscribed in a process of disappearance, of becoming invisible; on the other hand, the plastinates (completely drained of fluids in order to stop decomposition) are frozen in time, trapped in a state of complete exposure.

So far, Von Hagens's exhibitions have only taken place in Western countries – cultures obsessed with the progress of medicine, with keeping bodies in 'good' shape and with concealing the facts of aging and death (e.g. by means of plastic surgery). In these cultures, death is no longer part of life, let alone its completion. It has been forced out into special institutions, which themselves allocate particular spaces for it, often of little value: hospitals and their mortuaries. Seen from this perspective, the construction of the new Hôpital Européen Georges-Pompidou in Paris must have been the result of a bungled action. As a sign of our anxiety before death 'in flesh and bone,' the building plans did not include any space for the mortuary: in the end, it had to be built in the parking lot. The ethnologist Judith Wolf writes:

> Even today, the mortuary is often subject to double marginalization. On the one hand, as a space for the deceased it represents a place that everyone, staff or not, wants to keep away from. As soon as we are dealing with death, we find, in the hospital like anywhere else, reactions of refusal and denial, attitudes trying to either conjure or avoid the affair. I was surprised to see that in the hospitals I have visited, very few members of the staff were actually able to find the mortuary; some of them told me that they would never set foot in there. It is a world apart, often situated at the very end of the hospital (sometimes close to the rubbish bins), not always shown on the orientation plans and its telephone number is not listed with the other services. One symptomatic anecdote: a large, newly built Parisian hospital simply failed to include the mortuary in its architectural plans. Eventually it was built in the parking lot. On the other hand, the work of the mortuary seems to be, almost by nature, distant from the rest of the hospital's work. The hospital is indeed a place of care, entirely oriented towards the objective of recovery, of a return to health. In this framework, death can hardly fail to mark the failure of the whole enterprise.
>
> *(Wolf 2006)*

Von Hagens is trying to rise up to the same challenge – of doing away with death and its processes (decomposition) – by giving the dead a new identity in what must indeed be understood as a new body.

A ruling issued in France in September 2010 therefore concluded that '(…) the remains of the deceased must be treated with respect, dignity and decency – the exposition of dead bodies for commercial purposes fails to meet this criteria' (Court of Cassation 2010).[1] The verdict followed upon the exhibition 'Our Body à corps ouvert,' which was organised at the Espace 12 Madeleine, a center for the arts, education and science. The exhibition displayed plastinated bodies and human organs in different poses, in order to show the internal workings of the human body. The bodies used were Chinese cadavers. Two French NGOs, Together Against the Death Penalty and Solidarity China, together filed a complaint. According to Céline Fretel, Attorney at Law, the Paris Court of First Instance, the Paris Court of Cassation and the French Supreme Court all unanimously condemned the exhibition. The rulings were based on an article of the French Civil Code, which declares that 'the respect due to the human body does not cease with death. The remains of deceased persons, including ashes from the cremated body, must be treated with respect, dignity and decency.' Fretel emphasises the judges' uneasiness regarding this act of censorship, given that the exhibition was 'primarily' a cultural and artistic event.

> Art's vocation is to interrogate its viewer, even if it is by shocking him. The judges were asked to arbitrate between two principles: the respect due to the dead and to the human body (dead or alive) and the freedom of artistic creation. It seems that in its decision, the Supreme Court simplified the equation, leaving aside the question of creative freedom, which the case nonetheless does raise. By doing so, the judges did not rekindle the debate on censorship that had been provoked some years earlier by the publication of 'Rose bonbon' [a novel featuring pedophilia – trans. note] or by the [sexually explicit] exhibition 'Presumed innocent.' However, the affair shows that the concept of human dignity has become a criterion for delimiting artistic freedom.
>
> *(Fretel 2010)*

She continues:

> In their decision to ban 'Our Body à corps ouvert,' the judges did not refer to the objectification of the human body. It would have been difficult to use this characteristic of the living when dealing with something that the law already considers an [inanimate] object. The Court of Cassation ruled that the organisers must find out 'whether the living persons had consented to the use of their body.' Such consent would nonetheless have been inoperative and in no case justifies the offence against the respect due to the human person and body. Thus in the so-called 'dwarf-tossing' affair, where censorship did intervene, the persons used as projectiles had obviously given their consent.
>
> *(Fretel 2010)*

Fretel consequently asks the question of whether a corpse can legally be exhibited. According to the Court, which gave the example of the long-lasting exhibition of mummies, the answer is yes; however, it disapproved of the artistic manipulations to which the plastinated bodies were subject and which the Paris Court of First Instance overtly criticised: 'As far as one can judge, the cutting and dissecting caters to the spectacle, to virtuosity … in the resulting aestheticism the presentation of corpses and organs uses dissections that are not scientifically legitimate, as well as arbitrary coloring and unrealistic staging; in this regard it has clearly failed the standards of decency.' The Court's decision also drew on the prohibition against the marketing of human bodies. The 'corpse' presented in this way appears overexposed, showing at once the horror of death and the 'beauty' of the *mise-en-scène*. This clash of images (death/aesthetics) raises questions for the spectators as well as for legislators.

Not to do away with … death!

Based on this analysis, I would conclude that these bodies, dead and plastinated, are not corpses but imitations of living bodies, staged for the gaze of the visiting families and intended to show the immortality of physical being. What the organising institution (a museum or any other institution that legitimises these expositions) shows us is therefore a denial of death and an effort to preserve the 'good' form (as opposed to the absence of shape or form) in an effort to keep death at bay. The horror of the dying material body is unbearable – we must die cleanly, preserved in the odorless plastic, even if it means becoming a figure of spectacle. The pedagogical argument is untenable: the anatomy of the body can be perfectly reconstituted by computer graphics, using interactive features that can be equally attractive to young people. As regards the dissection of bodies practiced in medical schools, it is meant to educate students in the purest tradition, plus the bodies are then closed, instead of being exhibited in museums. Although I do not consider the plastinated bodies corpses (because they have been drained of fluids), the fact is that they originate from human corpses and have been transformed primarily for financial gain, rather than for pedagogical purposes. Von Hagens is making an image and a name for himself on account of the anxieties provoked by the absence of form, if not by sacrificing the dignity of executed prisoners (some of the plastinated bodies came from murdered Chinese convicts). The memory of the trafficking in human bodies, both alive and dead, carried out by the Nazis, who treated them as Stuk, as mere things, is still fresh. Perhaps we should not blame Von Hagens, but those who have allowed him to operate for the pleasure of our little darlings. (A word to the wise is enough.)

Note

1 I would like to thank Natalie Felzenszwalbe for bringing this ruling to my attention.

References

Albers, F. (1998) 'The longing called Identity,' in *[ID]entiteit* (Exhibition catalogue) Anvers.

Andrieu, B. (1994) *Les Cultes du Corps: Éthique et Sciences*. Paris: L'Harmattan.

Ardenne, P. (2006) *Extrême: Esthétique de la Limite Dépassée*, Paris: Flammarion.

Caillois, R. ([1939]1950) *L'Homme et le Sacré*, Paris: Gallimard.

Court of Cassation (2010) Ruling no 764 of 16 September 2010. Online. Available HTTP: <http://www.courdecassation.fr/jurisprudence_2/premiere_chambre_civile_568/764_16_17506.html> (accessed 6 September 2013).

Didi-Huberman, G. (1999) *Ouvrir Vénus: Nudité, Rêve, Cruauté*, Paris: Gallimard.

Fretel, C. (2010) L'arrêt 'Our body' du 16 septembre 2010. Village de la Justice. Online. Available HTTP: <http://www.village-justice.com/articles/arret-septembre-Celine-Fretel,8589.html> (accessed 6 September 2013).

Le Nouvel Observateur (2001) 'Les écorchés du docteur Von Hagens. Morts ou vifs?' 18 October, 2001.

Marion, G. (2004) Les cadavres 'plastinés' de von Hagens sont des condamnés à mort chinois, *Le Monde*, 20 January 2004.

National Public Radio (30 April 2001) All Things Considered. No. 8. 'Body Art.' Radio program. Available at: http://www.npr.org/templates/story/story.php?storyId=1122244 (accessed 6 September 2013).

Sicard, D. (2002) 'Le corps en pièces détachées. Enjeux scientifiques, économiques et philosophiques', *Les Tribunes de la Santé*, 1(6).

Vernant, J.-P. (2001) 'La mort ou les morts,' Autour des morts: mémoire et identité (Actes du Ve colloque international sur la sociabilité), Rouen: Université de Rouen.

Wolf, J. (2006) 'Les émotions dans le travail en milieu mortuaire: obstacle ou privilège?', *Face* À *Face 8*, 'Les politiques de l'intime'. Online. Available at: http://faceaface.revues.org/265?lang=en (accessed 6 September 2013).

13

OF BEAUTY AND 'BEAUTIES'

Female identities and body image in Colombia

Alcira Forero-Peña

Socioeconomic, cultural, and political background

'Colombian women are beautiful', or so I have sometimes heard from men and women in the US, European, and other Latin American countries. As a Colombian anthropologist, I know that my female fellow citizens are not more or less beautiful than women in other societies, since beauty is relative to many variables and the context is a key to understand what people mean and how physical 'beauty' is produced, re-constructed, consumed, and exchanged. I acknowledge a few from a long list of anthropologists who have produced a rich and large corpus of literature that conceptualises the human body cross-culturally.[1] Before discussing the 'body image' in Colombia I would like to problematise how this society presents more than one paradigm: being a rich country with plenty of human and natural resources, extreme forms of social inequality and violence prevail,[2] including structural violence (Farmer 2003) that can affect everyone in all societies, and violence against women. Undoubtedly, what is taken for granted in the global North, i.e. that the rule of law in a democratic society must be respected, doesn't apply in Colombia, at least not for the working poor, for the marginalised population, male and female. Colombian governments, past and present, often have assumed warrior-like and authoritarian rhetoric and actions with the justification of combating the guerrilla, the drug traffic or common crime. They are backed by very well-funded and huge military organisations and industries. Alongside the regular army, the society has suffered from the growing influence of parallel armies created by drug lords, the 'paramilitary' (irregular armies, often working in tandem with the regular one), guerrillas, and other private armies, whose massive resources, money, and lifestyle have had a deep impact on Colombians: millions are now uprooted and internally displaced. Further effects of these warring armies and environment include the reinforcement and distorted male-centered gender hierarchies, the [mis]constructions of women, women's bodies, as well as the notion of women's physical beauty.

In spite of the Colombian State's declared goal of countering the drug trade, its actions have actually strengthened the paramilitaries who have exercised extreme forms of violence and perpetrated unspeakable crimes against the civilian population, especially women. These crimes include, but are not limited to, *feminicides* or the killing of women in gruesome ways where they are tortured and their bodies are violated in multiple forms, just because they are women.[3] These armed actors have heightened the levels of violence notwithstanding the courageous resistance by social, popular, and women's movements seeking peace and justice, all denouncing Human Rights violations, crimes against humanity and women. Colombian society is still prey to violence and deadly agendas.

Some of the worst forms of globalisation, in the shape of drug trafficking producing trillions of dollars which are being laundered in the global North and South (including Colombia), are also part of the scenario. Entrepreneurs have set up a wide array of 'clean' businesses, including 'aesthetic medicine' and 'health tourism' in Colombia and other countries. To be sure, the money from the drug trade has not benefitted most of Colombians although investment in construction and war industries has resulted in some job creation. The growth of the informal sector of the economy that supplies all sorts of services and items to people, including the educated and shrinking middle class, is increasing. I would argue that this money has intensified conspicuous consumption, for those who can afford the high prices of desired, often imported commodities that become status symbols such as certain body images. More troubling, it has intensified the desire for all the objects that most people cannot purchase.

A volume of articles focusing on the relationship between bodies and inequalities in the Colombian context highlight the inevitability of two dyads: *body/image* and *body/machine*, two of the ways in which we are allowed to exist nowadays. We consume to create the first one with what the second receives for what it is able to produce, whatever it earns' (Viveros Vigoya and Garay Ariza 1999: 16–20).[4] Then, they take the reader into a journey, with their experiences as workers, in which the body suffers ill-treatment, in a city that is not kind to human beings, with a few exceptions such as their encounters with art and music. They underscore how from a very early age in people's lives, social mirrors emerge and with them their realisation of how they are classified according to their bodies: hair colour and texture, skin complexion or eye shape are grounds for labels and expectations, for assigned and expected statuses and roles. Their take on contextualisation is similar to mine: they are critical of where Colombia is located in the global world, and the impact this has on people and their bodies.

This socio-political and cultural environment produced a whole generation of *traquetos* or *sicarios*, the young drug-lords' henchmen who still thrive. They are merciless because of their early gender-based and other forms of socialisation in aggressive environments marked by the withdrawal of human kindness, displaying the utmost disrespect for human life in general and for women as human beings

– with, sometimes, the exception of their mothers. They are clear results and victims of structural violence and of 'La Violencia'.[5] In the drug traffic businesses they are paid comparatively high wages, in a country with very high rates of unemployment and poverty.[6] In spite of the official rhetoric about the success of *The Plan Colombia*, the *War on Drugs* programs, and the 'reinsertion' (the pretended surrender of arms by the irregular armed groups), the number of these young men is growing. And they have acquired the power and means to buy commodities, including young women.

These social actors have created a new 'aesthetics', a *Narcoestética*[7] as it refers to the drug lords' powerful influence, not only with their money but with their taste, on the whole country's perception of what is beautiful or not. Rincon (2009) described it in a very critical article on the subject: '[We] are a culture where anything goes if one stops being poor, where public discourses emphasise the need to show off and exhibit what one has acquired, if one is rich. There is just one method to acquire this culture: to have cash, weapons, silicone-women, strident music, flashy clothes and homes, together with many cars and objects' (Rincon 2009: 148).[8] This *aesthetics* has strongly influenced people's ideals of female beauty and body images so women are often highly sexualised, their physical attributes openly evaluated and seen as lacking. Large breasts are preferred and so women resort to surgical 'solutions' to their own faulty ones. And many women have followed suit by displaying their re-shaped bodies.

'Las Bellas Colombianas' (the Colombian 'Beauties'): beauty pageants, women's magazines, and TV shows

> Every father's dream was that his daughter would grow up to be a Miss Colombia.
>
> *(Paternostro 1998: 3)*

> Feeling the importance of being beautiful – beautiful as seen by our class – I followed all the rules. To be beautiful was to have blue eyes and blond hair, or at least straight hair. Dark curls like mine are too much a sign of mixed breeding, so I dreamt of having hair as straight as spaghetti.
>
> *(Paternostro 1998: 112)*

I remember growing up in Bogotá, leafing through or reading magazine articles and observing very carefully the many pages devoted to the photographs of the contestants in 'Señorita Colombia' (Ms Colombia) in Cartagena where the pageant still takes place. Likewise, every year, as a ritual, members of my family and friends who, like most of Colombians, were glued to the TV for hours following all possible details of Ms Colombia's participation in the Ms Universe pageant, rooting for her and feeling a national pride when she would make it to the finals. These sentiments and feelings are still experienced by people from what I have observed and colleagues have corroborated. But in Colombia there were and still are hundreds of beauty pageants and hundreds of 'queens', such as the Reina del Café

(The Queen of Coffee), the Queen of the Banana, the Queen of Cattle Raising, to name just a few. In each of these events the physical attributes of women are thus evaluated every day by everyone, men and women.

Interestingly, the Colombian state has been openly involved in marketing beauty as a national resource, not unlike natural resources.[9] As it happened, the first beauty pageant in Cartagena in 1934 helped welcome President Franklin D. Roosevelt and was meant to inaugurate foreign relations between the two countries. Together with incipient tourism, beauty pageants merged the marketing of regional differences and trade alongside women's bodies. Displayed women's bodies became a medium the state has used to enter the domain of heteronormative trade relations in which those exposed bodies were among the popular commodities and a key factor in the wealth of the nation (Schaeffer-Grabiel: 2006). The tourism industry and the media have fed into them extensively: one can see the posters of and articles about the 'beauty queens' all over.

In these pageants the advertising and manipulating of 'beauty' canons for women has plainly excluded for decades the very large Afro-Colombian population and the even larger Colombian *mestizo* population with pronounced indigenous phenotypes who, not surprisingly, do not belong to the upper or upper-middle class. This ensures entry to just the 'right' class and to the favoured phenotype, the one with heavily stereotypical European features: fair complexion, tanned but not too tanned, pointed nose, mirroring the mentioned canon and images for the body that for decades were judged by mostly men. If one looks at the famous Miss Universe or Miss World beauty pageants, one often finds a Colombian contestant in the finals. This tradition dates back over 50 years to when one Colombian young woman was crowned as Miss Universe in 1958 and the tradition goes on. In recent years, however, and mostly because of the proverbial desire to mimic what occurs in the US and Europe, some Afro-Colombian and other 'ethnic' young women, have gained entry to the pageants, just as a token.

The influence of soap operas/*telenovelas*

Writing about *telenovelas* as a form of cultural production in which the viewer is presented with 'apparently one dimensional characters and reductive plots…[that] mask a more complex and untidy interpretation of everyday reality that engages viewers in a process of self-identification with tropes representing the more complex realities of Latin American societies' (Benavidez 2008: 44). We are reminded that, after all, they are worth analyzing to fully understand the interplay between the viewers and their realities.

In Colombia, as in hundreds of societies, soap operas have become a staple in the daily lives of millions of people. Whenever I go visiting, I notice that at least in one room somebody is watching one. Also, I have acquired a repertoire of some of the most popular ones thanks to people who take the time to explain the plot, the actors' performance, and their popularity. It is not a coincidence that certain *telenovelas* that focus on women's appearance, beauty or the lack of it, have been produced in Colombia in recent years and have become a hit, nationally and internationally. As an example is the soap opera *Betty la Fea* or *Ugly Betty*, which was written and produced in Colombia, and became very popular in dozens of countries, finally being produced for US audiences. The storyline centres around a young woman whose looks (quite out of sync with the mainstream Colombian 'beauty' canon) and whose social class (lower-middle and working class), are both a challenge to her professional career in an environment that requires a certain body image and demeanor in the apparel and fashion design industries. So, in spite of being brainy, and of her professional training, her sense of justice and being a hard working young woman, she has to contend with the unethical, non-professional, upper-middle class 'beauties' as well as with men who find her insignificant in a literal sense, physically and socially. More importantly, she has to contend with the 'mainstream', hegemonic views on feminine beauty, with a culture of corruption at different levels, and extreme forms of sexism and classism. But the story takes a 'dramatic' turn when Betty evolves, little by little, from 'ugly duckling' into a beautiful swan, thus making fantasies real. At the end she looks very much like the standard and accepted 'beauty'. This is revealing of what the media messages convey. It is also telling how much the North American beauty ideal and body image continues to represent the ideal in many societies (Fedorak 2007).

Of *traquetos*, their money and 'their' women

Some of the most coveted commodities in the world of the *traquetos* mentioned before are young, 'pretty' women: 'hot babes' who they sometimes 'buy' quite cheaply. But the purchase seems to be conditioned on matching certain aesthetic expectations such as having big breasts. It seems that this is not unlike men in the US who have fantasised of women like Pamela Anderson and other more current 'bombshells' like her and like the successful Colombian actor Sofía Vergara, probably best known now as one of the actors in 'Modern Family', an ABC TV series.

The drug trade has flooded Colombia with commodities that most people cannot afford but desire nonetheless. It has given birth as well to thousands of the mentioned *traquetos/sicarios*, ready to die and do the 'dirty' tasks of killing, terrorising, and torturing those who oppose the power of the drug-tycoons, and ready to buy and use cheap and not-so-cheap young women to feel like *varones*, 'real men' or *machos*, and in control. It is not surprising then that given the social background presented above, women whose families have been broken by all forms of violence, both structural violence, a result of the armed conflict, and whose needs as citizens have not been met by the state, have sought transformations that cater for the demand. Their lack of economic autonomy and the many challenges to their struggle for survival and for individual agency have added extra burdens to their lives so they seek to ensure basic needs and other forms of security for them and their families by being picked by a man (or men?), although sometimes they seem to be very active in looking for the man/men they would be interested in. However, they must look attractive (increasingly blonde, tanned but not too tanned, fit, pointed nosed, with big and firm breasts, and prominent butts) and strive to gain currency in this aesthetics that is not constructed entirely by or for them – but to which they acquiesce and contribute nonetheless.

The goal for many women, mostly poor or lower-middle class and young ones, with no good paying job in sight, has become to achieve 'the perfect' body image and face and they have gone to great lengths to acquire that certain look of 'hot-babes', thanks to the growth of the so called 'cosmetic industry'. But despite its advertisements about the affordability of those 'miraculous' procedures, always eager to attract international customers,[10] for most Colombian women, the price to acquire these looks is too high, sometimes it could be their life itself.[11]

In real life, no doubt, there are many dissidents to this aesthetic: women whose bodies and physical attributes do not match the mentioned requirements and who are happy with them. Also, there are women who are happy not to be stereotyped, and so too their companions, lovers, husbands and wives. But here I am referring to tendencies.[12]

Of breast implants and silicone

Fine lingerie is one of Colombia's booming industries and you can find *Leonisa*, a well-known Colombian lingerie brand, in quite chic boutiques in Miami, New York, and some towns in New Jersey, but as Silvana Paternostro, a Colombian writer and journalist, writes in The Atlantic's article rightly entitled 'Drug Busts' (April 1, 2011) 'it is daunting to find an unpadded "bra" in Bogotá'. The reason is obvious to the reader: women there would 'prefer' to have them padded to look 'bustier' than they naturally are. Buying them is, obviously, cheaper than having an implant, and safer. Paternostro in her article highlights one of the first 'role models' for this trend: Natalia Paris, a famous model of intimate apparel and who is now a 'celebrity'. What she reveals to Paternostro in her interview should make one rethink what (or who) was behind Ms. Paris's 'taste': Is it the preference of the '*traquetos*' or is it the all-American male taste (or fixation?) for big breasts à la Pamela Anderson? Or both? Natalia Paris avows in the interview that this celebrity was her role model growing up and that her own mother, more than 20 years ago, paid for her breast implants for her eighteenth birthday after which her career as a model took off. Since then, thousands of Colombian girls as young as 15 years old are seeking the same kind of presents or ways to get the money to pay for them together with an array of other 'cosmetic surgeries' (Paternostro 2011).

It is no coincidence then that a very popular *telenovela* in Colombia a few years ago, *Sin Tetas No Hay Paraiso* (*Without Tits There Is No Paradise*), was about a flat-chested, poor teenager who wants to sell her virginity for a pair of implants and becomes a *pre-pago* or prostitute/escort for the petty and not so petty *traquetos*. The soap opera became a hit, in spite of the violence typical of the drug dealing mafias and it was bought by *Telemundo*, one of the big Spanish speaking channels in the US, and by ABC, airing it in the US to millions of 'Hispanics'. Here, we should think and rethink the role of the media in displaying these kinds of narratives and images about body images of women.

Besides the surgeries to improve the desired body image there has been an increasing number of other surgical procedures demanded, we are told, by women: surgeries of the female sex organs are on the rise and a surgical industry is growing in several countries that include Colombia which advertise such procedures under the general label of 'cosmetic surgeries'. They are also advertised as cheaper than those done in the 'developed' countries (Brumberg 1998). Pertaining to the surgeries' huge demand in Colombia, Tovar Rojas (2004) wrote 'Displaying diplomas from prestigious universities, the physicians, almost all male, impose their esthetics with the scalpel, widely advertising through the media 'corrective methods' and 'solutions' where 'perfect bodies' could be achieved. They also offer 'miracles', mostly for women, with the proverbial 'before' and 'after' pictures, selling the idea that a small bust is a 'disease' that the sufferer has to [be cured of] in the operating room' (Tovar Rojas 2004: 11–13).[13] One wonders whether women who undergo these procedures are enjoying themselves by the transformations that the mentioned creative and not-so-creative processes and procedures afford them in spite of the physical pain and risks they entail.

Colombian women's predicament

Caught up between the many demands that contemporary life presents them, Colombian working and lower-middle class women are facing many challenges, and survival is the most important one. Strategies to face the lack of financial capital have included for the majority of them working longer hours in menial jobs for very low wages in the midst of a society where conspicuous consumption is shamelessly displayed in the numerous and newly built malls – à l'Americaine – in all major cities as a result of money laundering enterprises and international investment, which have taken many forms and many markets. However, thousands of young and not-so-young women have resorted to 'using' men with access to cash to acquire desired commodities and unwittingly have ended up being used by them as mere objects and then being discarded afterwards, often hurt or even killed. It is true that a few of these women might attain some levels of empowerment, but they seem to be a minority.

The young women who subject themselves to breast implants and other 'cosmetic surgeries' and who engage in very unequal exchanges, including but not restricted to sex, are as much global products as the silicone breasts they carry, the commodities they buy after the exchanges, and the magazines, TV shows, and the Internet that carry stories about female celebrities. In so doing they are acting on a not-so-level playing field. Naïvely, they are trying to make fantasies real, aspiring to emulate the appeal of those 'celebrities'. Other women advertise their body images in newspapers, magazines, or the Internet in the hope of catching the attention of men worldwide who would rescue them from the drudgery and suffering that comes with the condition of poverty, low-level jobs or no job at all.

What I can see in these processes is the interplay of oppression and resistance within an intricate system, often open and obvious but sometimes subtle in gender, class, and 'racial' and ethnic relations. Susan Bordo (1993) writes: 'the human body is itself a politically inscribed entity, its physiology and morphology shaped by histories and practices of containment and control' (Bordo 1993: 21) and this idea encourages problematising the question of who controls who, where, and why. In these processes there is a convergence of different forms of oppression which is lived differently by different women. Complex and profound inequalities are created or worsened by the global economy within countries where wealth, power, education, social status, and material comfort are dramatically skewed. Another factor in this process is the *beauty* industry that for generations has catered to all women across class, culture, age, and ethnicity. To be sure, in Colombia and elsewhere there is a big emphasis on the body as a way of defining the self, so dieting, body sculpting, and mindful exercise and sports have all become signs of the times. But using the scalpel too 'freely' could be a dangerous business.

Clearly, by consenting to their disempowerment within seemingly 'free' exchanges by providing an attractive commodity in the form of the prescribed body image, and sex, women are gaining access to scarce resources like money and a different status in Colombia. The devaluation of women's contribution to the labor force and the lack of job opportunities that match their training and/or their aspirations have left many women with just a few options: one of them is the sale of their bodies. In so doing, many are selling their soul. While I don't want to evoke the image of 'enslaved' or completely powerless women here, my aim is to raise a cautionary voice about the blessings of globalisation and capitalism where even the most sacred – in this case, predominantly, the female body – melt into thin air and, and tragically, many lose their lives. In these processes middle-class women are not exempt from those dangers. They fear losing their partners to younger and prettier women and also undergo 'cosmetic surgeries'.

Finally, Colombian State policies funded by terror and war, have intensified the effects of violence, leaving entire populations with nothing to live on, except their bodies, bodies that are treated as disposable and consumable and so they are buried or worked upon in the operating room and the *narco*'s kitschy villas and apartments. The struggle for social and economic rights, for women and men alike, seems to me one that must be supported together with more specific struggles for gender equality and women's rights because the processes leading to egregious disregard for women's dignity and equality in Colombia are tightly linked to those that have led men, old and young, to take up the weapons and assert their sense of masculinity by hurting women and joining the many armies in protracted violent conflict with deep roots in social inequality and structural violence.

There are several questions that should be asked as they refer to what I have presented here. One of them is to what extent body image influences Colombian women's self-confidence, and if they really and freely accept the cited dehumanising procedures and activities and commoditisation of bodies and lives. Many Colombian women, and men, are challenging the *status quo*, the 'normative category' of beauty, who are fighting for human rights and against violence towards women. So, in spite of the grim realities that I write about, I can see many dissidents of the described processes, a certain assertiveness, and other more independent attitudes regarding women's body images and the construction of femininity. But it is an ongoing uphill struggle.

Acknowledgements

First of all, I would like to thank Dr. Ekaterina Sukhanova who organised the International Conference on Body Image at CUNY Graduate Center in the spring of 2011 and invited me to join a panel and later on to contribute a chapter to this collective volume on Body Image. Thanks are due to my colleagues at LaGuardia Community College's Writing Seminar, Profs. Danielle Insalaco-Egan, Patricia Sokolsky, Habiba Boumlik, and Suzanne Uzzilia for their support, suggestions, and sharp questions. To professors Patricia Tovar and Marietta Saravia-Shore for their equally crucial help. To my friends, Deirdre Mahoney, Dr. John Steen and Richard Lefkowitz, who read and commented on my draft a word of appreciation. As usual, I assume responsibility for any errors.

Notes

1 For a thorough and sharp review and contribution to the subject, see Das (1996), Halliburton (2002), Mascia-Lees and Sharpe (1992), Sault (1994), Scheper-Hugues and Lock (1987).

2 'Violence committed by configurations of social inequalities that, in the end, has injurious effects on bodies similar to the violence of a stabbing or a shooting' (Holmes 2013: 43).

3 Sanford (2008), Gartner et al. (2001) and others have written extensively about this social phenomenon as it occurs in Guatemala, Mexico, Colombia, and elsewhere.

4 My translation.

5 The so-called 'Violencia' (or Violence) in Colombia is a long process that dates back several decades with deep roots in extreme forms of social inequality. This is the reason for what several scholars have called the 'lost generations'. Sanchez and Meertens (2001), Meertens and Segura-Escobar (1997), Tovar Rojas (2004), and Meertens (2012) are some of the researchers who have done excellent work on the subject.

6 For revealing data, such as the Inequality-Adjusted Index (IHDI), Multidimensional Poverty Index (MPI) and Gender Inequality Index (GII), see the Human Development Report 2013 for Colombia from the UNDP. They display very clear-cut patterns of concentration of wealth and growing poverty.

7 The expression refers to a notion of beauty in the context of unbelievable amounts of cash that the drug lords manage as well as corrupt politicians, big landowners, entrepreneurs, and their henchmen. For a better understanding of the concept, Rincón (2009) provides insights and illustrations for the Colombian context.

8 My translation. Interestingly, this author goes beyond problematising the concept and behaviours attached to it: he sees a clear connection of *narcoestética* with practices and taste of the local bourgeoisie.

9 Just to make sure, the Colombian state is not the exception in these types of endeavors. For an anthropological and incisive take on beauty pageants see Wilk (1995).

10 Websites with enticing advertisements, photographs, YouTube videos, and narratives such as 'Plastic Surgery in Paradise' referring to a private clinic in Cartagena, a city in the

Caribbean. All this is pretty similar to the advertisements and demand for plastic surgeries in France and abroad, such as Tunisia. For the sake of cross-cultural comparison, see a recent issue of the French weekly *Le Point* with the cover title 'Le livre noir de la medicine esthétique' that includes an interesting interview to Georges Vigarello's 'L'apparence physique, veritable quête du Graal' (September 26, 2013, No. 2141:40-51).

11 I came across several articles in newspapers about fatal results for women while undergoing plastic surgery. Many quack doctors have opened 'clinics' that do not meet basic, scientific and professional standards. In fact, Tovar Rojas (2004) mentions how some young women injected their bodies with cooking oil to change their buttocks with the obvious devastating consequences. This anthropologist also cites several cases of the deaths of young women due to surgeries gone wrong.

12 In Colombia (and elsewhere), some working-class men have expressed their preference for '*las gorditas*' or the little chubby ones, for different aesthetic and erotic reasons whose deep roots should be further researched. In India, where I lived for more than 3 years, people in general, again not the upper class, tend to prefer women who are not so thin: it would symbolise, for them, that these women's families are not poor, that they can feed their daughters well.

13 Tovar Rojas (2004) – my translation.

References

Benavides, H. (2008) *Drugs, Thugs, and Divas: Telenovelas and Narco-Dramas in Latin America*. Austin: Texas University Press.

Bordo, S. (1993) *Unbearable Weight: Feminism, Western Culture and the Body*. Los Angeles: University of California Press.

Brumberg, J. (1998) *The Body Project: An Intimate History of American Girls*. New York: First Vintage Book Edition.

Brumberg, J. (2007) 'Breast buds and "training" bra', in S. Shaw and J. Lee (eds), *Women's Voices, Feminist Visions. Classic and Contemporary Readings*. New York: McGraw Hill.

Das, V. (1996) 'Language and the body: transactions in the construction of pain', *Daedalus* 125(1, Social Suffering): 67–91.

Farmer, P. (2003) *Pathologies of Power: Health, Human Rights, and the New War on the Poor*, Berkeley: University of California Press.

Fedorak, S.A. (2007) *Anthropology Matters*. Peterborough: Broadview Press.

Gartner, R., Dawson, M., and Crawford, M. (2001) 'Women killing: intimate femicide in Ontario, 1974–1999', in D. Russell and R. Harmes (eds), *Femicide in Global Perspective*, New York: Teachers College Columbia University Press.

Halliburton, M. (2002) 'Rethinking anthropological studies of the body: Manas and Bodam in Kerala', *American Anthropologist* 104(2): 1123–1134.

Holmes, S. (2013) *Fresh Fruit, Broken Bodies: Migrant Farmworkers in the United States*, Berkeley: University of California Press.

Le Point (2013) 'Le livre noir de la medicine esthétique', September 26, 2013, No. 2141: 40–51.

Mascia-Lees, F.E. and Sharpe, P., eds. (1992) *Tatoo, Torture, Mutilation, and Adornment: The Denaturalisation of the Body in Culture and Text*, Albany: State University of New York Press.

Meertens, D. and Segura-Escobar, N. (1997) 'Uprooted lives: gender, violence, and displacement in Colombia.' *Singapore Journal of Tropical Geography*, 17(2): 165–178. Also published online: 26 AUG 2006, DOI: 10.1111/j.1467-9493.1996.tb00091.x

Meertens, D. (2012) 'Forced displacement and gender justice in Colombia: Between disproportional effects of violence and historical justice. Brookings –LSE project on Internal Displacement'. Online. Available HTTP: <http://www.brookings.edu/~/media/Projects/idp/tj%20case%20studies/Meertens%20Gender%20and%20Colombia.pdf>.

Paternostro, S. (1998) *In the Land of God and Man: A Latin Woman's Journey*. New York: Plume.

Paternostro, S. (2011) 'Drug busts. Colombia's reigning narco-babe seeks to lower her profile', *The Atlantic* (11 April).

Restrepo, L. (2004) *Delirio* Madrid: Santillana (US edition published 2007 as *Delirium* by Vintage, New York).

Rincón, O. (2009) 'Narco-estética y narco. Cultura en narco.lombia', *Nueva Sociedad* 222.

Sánchez, G. and Meertens, D. (2001) *Bandits, Peasants, and Politics: The Case of 'La Violencia' in Colombia* (translated by Alan Hynds). Austin: University of Texas Press.

Sanford, V. (2008) 'From genocide to feminicide: Impunity and human rights in twenty-first century Guatemala', *Journal of Human Rights* 7: 104–122.

Sault, N. (1994) 'The human mirror', in N. Sault (ed.) *Many Mirrors: Body Image and Social Relations*, New Brunswick: Rutgers University Press, pp. 1–28.

Schaeffer-Grabiel, F. (2006) 'Planet-love.com: cyberbrides in the Americas and the transnational routes of U.S. masculinity', *Signs: Journal of Women in Culture and Society*, 30(2, winter).

Scheper-Hugues, N. and Lock, M. (1987) 'The mindful body: a prolegomenon to the future work in medical anthropology', *Medical Anthropology Quarterly* 1: 6–41.

Tovar Rojas, P. (2003) 'La familia en tiempos de la guerra y la guerra dentro de la familia', in P. Tovar Rojas (ed.) *Familia, Género y Antropología. Desafíos y Transformaciones*. Bogotá: Instituto Colombiano de Antropología e Historia.

Tovar Rojas, P. (2004) 'El cuerpo subordinado y politizado. Reflexión crítica sobre género y antropología médica', *Revista Colombiana de Antropología* (40). Bogotá: Instituto Colombiano de Antropología e Historia.

UNDP (2013) 'Human Development Report for Colombia', Online. Available HTTP: <http://hdrstats.undp.org/images/explanations/COL.pdf>. Accessed 20 November 2013.

Vigarello, G. (2012) *La Silhouette, Du XVIIIe Siècle À Nos Jours. Naissance D'un Défi*, Paris: Seuil.

Vigarello, G. (2013) 'L'apparence physique, veritable quête du graal'. *Le Point*, September 26, 2141: 40–51.

Viveros Vigoya, M. and Garay Ariza, G. (eds.) (1999) *Cuerpo, Diferencias y Desigualdades*. Facultad de Ciencias Humanas, Universidad Nacional. Colección CES (Centro de Estudios Sociales).

Wilk, R. (1995) 'The local and the global in the political economy of beauty: from Miss Belize to Miss World', *Review of International Political Economy*, 2(1): 117–134.

14

TATTOOS/HYSTERIA

Jeanne Wolff Bernstein

Humans have marked their bodies with tattoos for thousands of years. These permanent designs – sometimes plain, sometimes elaborate, always personal – have served as amulets, status symbols, declarations of love, signs of religious beliefs, adornments, and they have at the same time also served as forms of punishment and kinship identifications. Tattoos are markings on the body which carry private and public messages, evoking sensory and symbolic renderings. They play with time and space, being fixed in the bodily skin while being ephemeral in their visual encounter with the Other.

Tattoos have existed for a long time and have gone through a diverse and fascinating history, spanning the gamut of being a mark of high distinction to becoming a sign of identifying criminals and branding prisoners in Nazi concentration camps.

The earliest tattoo dates back to Oetzi, the Iceman, whose frozen remains were found in 1991 in the Austrian/Italian alps. Dating back to 3300 BC, Oetzi bore 57 separate tattoos, consisting of simple dots and lines on his lower spine, left knee and

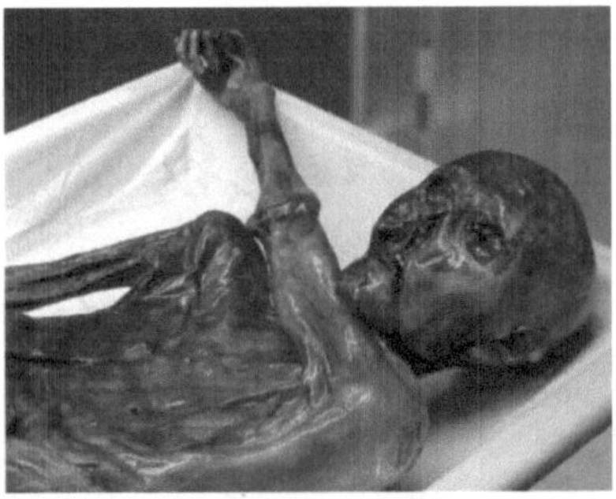

FIGURE 14.1

right ankle. According to the most recent research, it is believed that Oetzi used these tattoos as medical treatment to reduce pain. However, until Oetzi was discovered in 1991, the earliest known examples of tattoos on actual human bodies were thought to be of Egyptian origin, present primarily on several female mummies dating back to c. 2000 BC.

Greeks, on the other hand, used tattoos for communication among spies who would communicate their rankings and secret messages through their bodily markings. Romans, conversely, used tattoos primarily as a tool to identify criminals and slaves, often directly inscribing the price they paid for their slaves into their bodies. In Japan, for instance, centuries later, tattoos were used to mark officially the length of a prison sentence.

First offenses were marked with a line across the forehead. A second crime was marked by adding an arch, and a third line was marked by another line. Together these marks formed the Japanese character for 'dog', which in turn may have led to the current penal sentence 'Three strikes and you are out'.

Tattooing has been practiced for centuries in many cultures, particularly in different parts of Asia, yet it was William Dampher, a British sailor, exploring the South Seas, who was the first Westerner to bring back a fully tattooed man to London, by the name of Prince Giolo. Giolo was put on exhibition, making money for his discoverer, becoming a sensation for the London public. One hundred years later, in 1766, Captain Cook reinvigorated this rage when he brought back another fully tattooed man, by the name of Omai who, in turn, inspired many Westerners to inscribe discreet tattoos into their bodies. For a short period of time, tattoos began to function as signs of high distinction as the British upper class – much like today's upper middle classes – designated intimate parts of their bodies be permanently pigmented by visual designs. Captain Cook was also the first to transmit the meaning of the word 'tattoo' to the Western world. In Tahitian language, 'tatau' means 'to strike' and/or 'to mark' something. Cook was fascinated by the practice of tattooing, noting in his diary that 'Both sexes paint their bodies, Tattow, as it is called in their language. This is done by inlaying the colour of black under their skins, in such a manner as to be indelible.' He brought back with him seamen and sailors who had undergone the tattooing procedure, a tradition that would soon become associated with marine life in the public's mind. Images of the tropical world and exotic women would decorate sailors' arms and shoulders, forever reminding them of past adventures and lost loves. At the same time as tattoos became associated with marine lives, the British Royal Court also became fascinated with the visual depictions of tattoos and, over a short period of time, other kings from Norway, Denmark, Romania, Germany and Yugoslavia were joining the British crown, in espousing ornate tattoos on their bodies.

After the second world war, the art of tattooing became denigrated in the West, being primarily identified as a mark of low life, delinquency and criminal connections. An outbreak of hepatitis in the early 1960s in the US put a temporary stop to this culturally and historically rich practice. However, nowadays, tattooing has enjoyed a new renaissance and has become once again a socially reputable practice across many classes, while at the same time remaining a distinct mark of disenfranchised groups of people, primarily gang members who use tattoos to strike a common bond and to speak a common language. How can we understand this bodily art and the resurgence of the body as a live canvas and forge, in addition, a connection to Freud's theory of hysteria?

In the case of Cecile M., Freud notes that the hysteric 'creates a somatic expression for an emotionally colored idea by symbolization'(Freud 1905) which has to do with the fact the hysteric creates a particular link between the body and the word. He writes, when the hysteric expresses a verbal expression literally such as feeling 'a stab in the heart' or 'a slap in the face', the hysteric is not taking liberties with words, but is simply revealing once more the sensations to which the verbal expression owes its justification. The hysteric embodies her words and lives them out in her body. Much like the individual inscribing tattoos in her body, the hysteric also uses her body as a canvas upon which she enacts her unconscious and conscious phantasies. In her 2010 book, *Under the Skin: A Psychoanalytic Study of Body Modifications*, Allessandra Lemma, a British psychoanalyst, identifies three major phantasies which range from 'being one's own creator' to 'being a perfect match phantasies' to 'reclaiming parts of one self phantasies … These phantasies are felt to be necessary to the psychic equilibrium of individuals for whom body modifications have acquired a more compelling quality' (Lemma 2010: 5) If the tattoo is not just a simple decoration on the body but becomes an emblem imprinted all over the body, the question emerges to what extent a tattoo speaks the individual's desire and serves as a permanent mark to an internally felt psychic conflict? As we know from psychoanalytic infant studies, the baby's body is a mutually inscribed scene between the mother's unconscious sexual desire and the baby's sensualities, the mother's erotic, cuddling touches and the baby's erotogenic zones. In the *Three Essays on Sexuality*, Freud describes the skin as 'the erotogenic zone *par excellence*' since it embodies the sexual instinct involving pain and cruelty (Freud, 1905: 169). Thus the body always bears the history and the traces of the M/other since it is through the mother's desire – mediated by the father's desire – that the baby discovers his/her own desire. Through her touch and gaze, the mother invests the baby's body with her own libidinal desires and stirrings. Lemma writes, 'in order to feel desirable we are dependent on the other's libidinal cathexis of our body self…, and on the other's desire for us' (2010: 26). A key point of Lacan's theory also points to this psychic truth that the subject locates his own desire through the desire of the Other. Through the tactile and visual exchanges between mother and baby, the baby discovers his/her own desirability or undesirability and develops a body image that is profoundly shaped by the desire or lack thereof by the Other.

Now the hysteric is an acute chronicler of the M/other's enigmatic messages, receiving mixed messages about her own desirability. In *Hysteria* (2000), Bollas writes that the mother of a hysteric

> substitutes sound and performance for maternal love, giving the child a scene of a mother's love, in which portrayal substitutes for embodied

> mothering.... The hysteric is taking in a performance that is the mother's repudiated, yet partially realised, desire. Her symptoms then become scenes, events to which the hysteric bears witness in a dissociated way.
>
> *(Bollas 2000: 109, 111)*

The hysteric's characteristic ability to convert unwanted affects and incompatible ideas into symptoms, transforms her into the bearer of the M/other's censored history. Bollas goes on to explain that

> the hysteric shows off the self, transforming it into an event ready for inspection by the other. The stance expresses the self's arrest, or fixation, at the point when mother's language and child's sexuality are meant to fuse, in the acquisition of words that one can live with and which are psychically transformative. The hysteric shows us that s/he cannot accept the link between the body's expressed sexuality and the other's worded desire of it. It must be shown again and again.
>
> *(2000: 51)*

The tattoo just does that, it shows its invited spectators again and again the Other's warded off desire. That which could not be expressed, shows up now on rather than in the body. Don Hardy, a legendary San Francisco tattoo artist, calls the body 'the canvas that talks back' and in so doing, suggests that the tattooed body becomes a moving spectacle that arrests, accuses, warns, implores or seduces the Other into registering messages which could not be heard and seen before.

The desire to use one's own body as a canvas instead of a stretched framed canvas also suggests the desire to force spectators into a visual dialogue which they may not select on their own, transforming them into casual, possibly uncomfortable, yet also potentially curious voyeurs. Like the hysteric, the tattooed individual seeks to invade and provoke the Other in order to find out – without saying of course – who s/he is for his/her spectators. In line with my argument that the modern-day tattoo possibly represents our latest bodily 'conversions', in other words, our latest hysterical manifestations, I think that the tattoo functions likewise as a symbolic message sent into the space of the Other through which the bearer of the tattoo receives a response that in turn helps in shaping his/her identity. Since thinking about tattoos for this paper, I have occasionally trespassed the unspoken prohibition to inquire about tattoos when I see them on salesgirls' arms, bartenders' shoulders or students' necks and/or friend's legs. At first, most seemed surprised that I would ask such an 'intimate' question. However, everyone gradually revealed the source(s) of their choices for their tattoos. For many it just seemed an image they liked, a peace symbol, a Chinese symbol for happiness, the name of a loved or lost one like two sisters who had lost their father and had a blue jay feather inscribed in their arms to remember him. For one young woman, the music and pencil on her finger represents her 'spirit' and what is important to her and as she said, 'a need to have it on my body to make it more a part of me like literally, as kind of a reminder not to lose myself'.

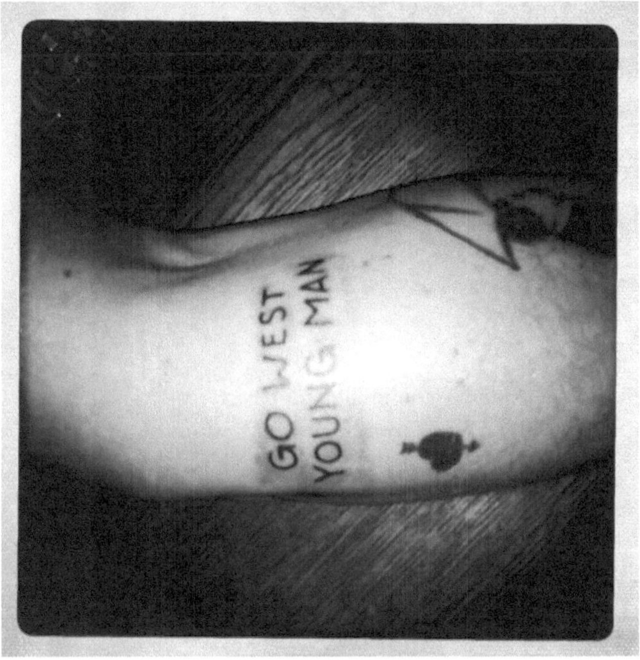

FIGURE 14.2

For another young man, imprinting 'Going West' into his arm served as a permanent reminder of a new direction he had chosen to take to change his life. For others, the tattoo represented a public acknowledgement of gratitude for their private suffering as they revealed themselves to be survivors of accidents or severe illnesses. They had marked the end of their pain with symbols of regeneration – such as a rising sun – or the dates of their recovery. What was striking to me, was that so many of the tattooed individuals were ready to reveal spontaneously the name of 'their' tattoo artist who had painted the images upon their bodies. In these descriptions, an intimate bond was gradually struck to the very person to whom they had submitted their body to receive their wished-for visual inscription(s).

The relationship between the tattoo artist and his bodily canvas is built upon trust and closeness and readily invokes parallels to the transference relationship the hysteric is inclined to construct to her analyst. According to Lacan, the hysteric does not identify with her lack but points towards the lack in the Other, always looking for the master over whom she can eventually reign. She gives herself to the master with all her body in pain and in so doing becomes his phallus/muse.

If we take one step back into history and look at the famous photographs of the hysterics collapsing into the arms of Dr. Martin Charcot, aren't some of us reminded of the poses tattooed women and men adopt to receive their tattoos from their masters? Akin to the hysteric's frequent visits to the hospital 'to use her body – as ailment presented to the loving other (the doctor now being a figure who tends

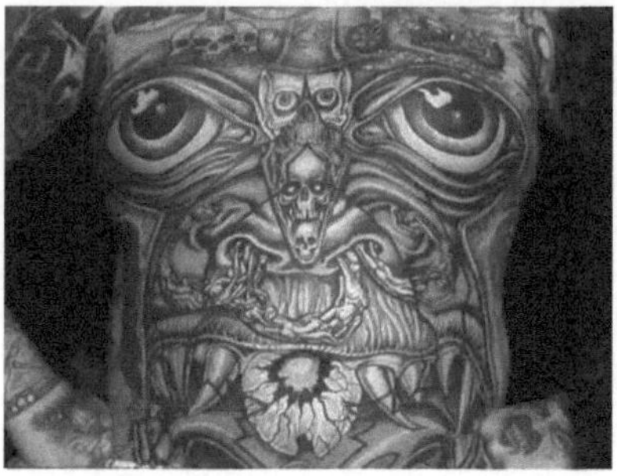

FIGURE 14.3

to bodies out of love), we may comprehend the hysteric's constant visits to hospital as a continual call to the mother to take the self back into care, and to rediscover the infant's body as something now desirable' (Bollas 2000: 59). If we replace the position of the analyst with that of the tattoo artist, we can see that the tattooed individual uses her body as an occasion for love to reinscribe the mother's rejection of her own sexuality. The hysteric finds in the tattoo artist's attentions a hand and a gaze that seems much more alive to the body's desires than that of the mother.

Visits, sometimes frequent visits to the tattoo salon may then end up serving as means of rewriting the individual's early history, of un- and re-wording the rejected desire left in the body by the Other, thus finally fulfilling the phantasy that a tattooed body can give birth to a new, more desirable and ultimately self-fashioned self.

In the end, the tattoo – much like the symptom – marks the Other and lashes out at the Other, combining in one stroke the memorialisation of past losses with the desire to punish the Other, forcing him into the role of being the witness bearing the pains of past inflictions and repressed memories.

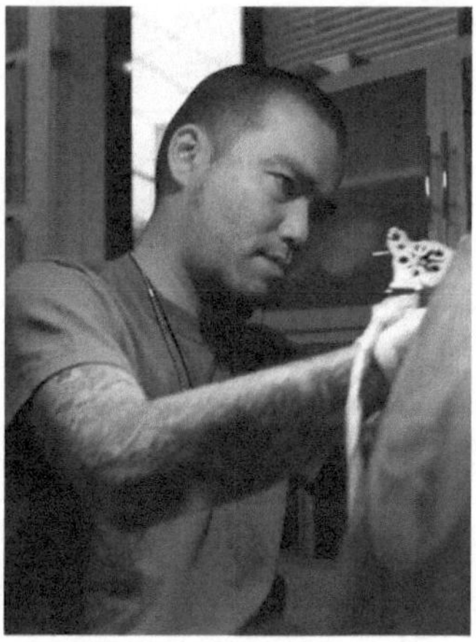

FIGURE 14.4

References

Bollas, C. (2000) *Hysteria*, London, New York: Routledge.

Freud, S. (1893) *Studies on Hysteria*, The Standard Edition of the Complete Psychological Work of Sigmund Freud, translated by A. Strachey & A. Tyson, Volume II, London: The Hogarth Press.

Freud S. (1905) *Three Essays on Sexuality*, The Standard Edition of the Complete Psychological Work of Sigmund Freud, translated by A. Strachey & A. Tyson, Volume VII, London: The Hogarth Press.

Lemma, A. (2010) *Under the Skin*, London, New York: Routledge.

15

BODY IN ART AND ART THERAPY

Humorous presentations

Alexander Kopytin

Introduction

Humour was quite often a subject of scrutiny in cultural-anthropological and social studies. It can be recognised as a significant human phenomenon with a far-reaching potential for grasping the nature of humans and how they relate to the world and themselves. It has many valuable functions that help people to better adapt to the natural and social surroundings, to cope with stressful situations and further reveal their creative potential. It has strong connections to the powerful inner and outer dynamics that take place in the human psyche and body as well as in interpersonal relations, across different institutions and societies. As such, humour can provide both healing and destructive effects.

Throughout the last decades, different manifestations of humour were recognised as important characteristics of either mental health, or pathology (Roux & Laharie 1998; Verdeau-Pailles 1998). Also its significant role in psychotherapy was emphasised (Ijuin 1998; Jakab 1998a, 1998b; Nagy 1998). At the same time connections between humorous body expressions represented in concrete actions, mimicry, or artistic productions of clients and therapeutic and clinical dynamics were not sufficiently explored. The paradox is that while there is an abundant literature commenting on the significance of the body-centered interventions in therapy (Damascio 1999; Feldenkrais 1950; McDougal 1989; Reich 1972), on the one hand, and the role of humour in psychotherapy and art therapy (Ijuin 1998; Jakab 1998a, 1998b; Nagy 1998), on the other hand, publications exploring complex correlations between humour, body and therapeutic dynamics are absent.

My interest in this subject was stimulated by the rich and multifaceted manifestation of humour in its strong connection to the physical body and its visual representations in art therapy and in art at large. I am enthusiastic about exploring diagnostic, predictive and therapeutic aspects of 'the humorous body' in psychotherapy and art therapy as well as in everyday life. I believe that our sense of humour is mostly body-centered. It can be induced, revealed and organised through various body expressions especially when they become a part of interpersonal and social matrix. A wide range of humorous reactions can be triggered, experienced, and objectified through art. Humour must be embodied and it must be artistically performed in one way or another and become a 'behavior of art' (Dissanayake 1988), in order to properly reveal its human nature and evoke different effects in us. Body as a site of powerful energies and drives must become 'an artistic channel' so that paradoxes and conflicts of our human nature can be transgressed and 'alchemically' transformed into the unified whole thanks to an element of humour.

Defining humour and its relation to body from the developmental and clinical perspective

Humour defined from the developmental perspective

Humour is a complex psychological and interpersonal phenomenon involving both emotions and cognitions, the conscious and the unconscious mind as well as the human body. It has a strong relation to our inner creative and sexual drives. It can be constructive or destructive, healthy or pathological depending on many factors.

Various definitions of humour and its different kinds including wit, joke, clowning, irony, sarcasm and cynicism exist. Different types of humour help to deal with specific objectives. Some types of humour are openly sexual and provide liberation of instinctual drives. Other types of humour help to express disagreement or even aggression against a person, or social or political obstacles. Very often, humour helps to defuse anxiety and suffering. Irony is different from other types of humour, because it deals not with unconscious repressed material, but rather with conscious aggressive ideas. Irony is a paradoxical intervention, which provides destructive effects with regard to the opponent. Humour and laughter may be involved when people are resistant to social powers. They may be signaling dominance or submission, rejection, or acceptance. Collective laughter has group-building power.

All categories of humour have common attributes, but there are important differences between them, too. Jakab (1998a) believes that humour is similar to metaphor:

> It has disguised, but understandable meaning… . Humour is a state of mind, a tendency to see hidden meanings and connections of repressed emotions and concepts transforming them into acceptable liberating presentations… . There are similarities between jokes and dreams. Each…works with condensation and displacement and indirect representation. However there is regression in dream, while there is no regression in jokes.
>
> *(p. 16)*

If humour is perceived through the lenses of the developmental theory it can become obvious that a certain level of conscious capability and ego formation is required to be able to understand and use humour in one's relationships with oneself and others. While certain humorous reactions appear early enough in children, when they play and interact with each other and adults a more sophisticated sense of humour is characteristic of the more mature stages and reflect the intellectual development from concrete to abstract thinking as well as increased ego complexity and self-perception.

I. Jakab (1998b) believes that humour can vary from developmentally more primitive laughing reactions of 3-year-old children evoked by concrete actions, to the more subtle experience of humour evoked or expressed through words and art, because 'understanding of humour and, especially, the difference between understanding concrete and abstract humour depends on the intellectual maturity' (p. 78).

Furthermore, the ability to understand and produce humour is also related to the level of psychological integrity of a person, the emotional security provided by the appropriate level of self-acceptance and self-understanding especially, as far as self-irony is concerned: 'To laugh at others requires less intellectual or emotional maturity than to laugh at one's self. Children usually suffer when the joke is on them, if they do not have the emotional security of solid self-esteem' (ibid, p. 78).

One of the core characteristics of humour is that it enables a person to dissociate with certain inner physical or mental qualities, to transgress them, on the one hand, and associate with them reaching the point of their reintegration, on the other hand: 'Humor looks at the self from the outside, from a distance. It sees problems... repressed feelings...taboos...and transfers them into acceptable properties of the self (acknowledging their existence as part of the self), although not overtly identifying with them' (Jakab 1998a: 17–18).

While undergoing the ego formation process and various developmental stages characterised by the growing differentiation of the self-perception, an individual typically performs an act of dissociation and reintegration not just once, but many times. In most cases a confrontation with the body as a representational vehicle of dissociated and reintegrated qualities takes place whenever an individual attains a new level of maturity; often, this process is accompanied with humour.

From the psychoanalytical viewpoint, the body and its manifestations are often perceived as a representation of the unconscious drives and functions in their uneasy connection to consciousness and super ego structures. This creates an inner tension in the ego, which is simultaneously shielding itself from the body, on the one hand, and resisting a temptation to re-unite itself with the body, on the other hand.

The paradox is that as it was established by S. Freud (Freud 1961b), the 'ego is first and foremost a bodily ego' (p. 26), in that the biological-instinctual infrastructure is the basis for the formulation of drives, which determine human motivations, behaviors and interactions. He also emphasised the role of muscular activity as one of the factors supporting ego formation and its ability to discriminate between inner and outer reality, since 'the perceptual...organism will...have found in the efficacy of its muscular activity a basis for distinguishing between an outside and an inside' (Freud 1961a: 119).

Thus, certain connections can be proposed, between the growing ability of the ego to defend and dissociate itself from the body as the biological-instinctual infrastructure and the aptitude of the ego to use humour as an instrument of dissociation from those structures, while retaining certain relations with them to provide psychosomatic (mental-physical) integration. Since sexuality and aggression constitute the most vital biological-instinctual functions realised through the body, the human need to dissociate and reintegrate with these functions is ever-present, but very differently expressed depending on the developmental level and other factors including clinical characteristics of the person and social-cultural norms.

In this context one's ability to feel and produce humour related to the body can be a reflection of a complex inner dynamic that involves sexuality and aggression as well as other drives. This dynamic embraces conscious and non-conscious, somatised manifestations that belong to both early (preserved by the body) and more recent, socially organised experiences in their interchange with each other. Therefore it's natural that physical markers of sexuality and aggression very often serve as powerful triggers of humour. At the same time, according to A. Ziv (1984), humour provides a wide spectrum of various effects, such as inclusion in the social context, non-destructive expression of aggression and sexuality, psychological defense and intellectual digestion of information. The facilitating role of humour in revealing creative forces of the psyche and providing space to play with oneself and reality should also be emphasised.

The role of art cannot be overestimated with this regard, because different body representations as correlates of dynamic inner constellations of mental and somatic, conscious and non-conscious processes related to basic and more recent drives and aspirations (creative activity, self-realisation and self-acceptance etc.) can be effectively revealed and realised though art (together with other expressive means).

Humour defined from the clinical-psychiatric perspective

In order to better understand diagnostic, predictive and therapeutic functions of humour, its relation to mental health and pathology should be further considered. Though humour in general is sometimes considered to be 'an essential part of mental health' (Jakab 1998b: 77), different kinds of humour can correlate both with mental health and various mental disorders. It is difficult to define, what, on the one hand, healthy humour is, and on the other hand, pathological or morbid humour is, since context plays a significant role. However, Judith Nagy (1998) believes that healthy, constructive humour helps make the borders of the self flexible in fighting problematic inner or outer situations, while pathological or destructive humour is correlated with destructive aggression, 'with the lack of the contact making ability and the rigidity of the borders of the ego. It can appear in the shape of sarcasm and irony' (p. 257).

More severe pathology is often linked to destructive and self-destructive humour. In cases of psychotic conditions humour as a significant regulative mechanism related to defenses and coping strategies appears to be less efficient and to have less therapeutic potential compared to stress-related, somatoform and neurotic mental disorders. I. Jakab (1998a) claims that for a psychotic person, humour may be too threatening and cannot alleviate symptoms. Schizophrenic patients have a different sense of humour from the so-called average person:

> Their humor consists frequently of irony and may be so idiosyncratic that the listeners do not understand them. Paranoid persons cannot accept humor; they interpret it as aggression. Patients in a manic state have no real sense of humor although they may tell a chain of jokes.
>
> *(p. 18)*

She believes that humour may be more functional and play a significant therapeutic role in neurotic patients and therefore must be supported and often interpreted throughout therapy.

G. Bengesser (1998) comments on the lacking sense of humour in some psychopaths. He claims that 'no system delineates a kind of psychopathy, in which humorlessness is the name-giving feature; but often it is constituting a feature of that kind of psychopathy … that is called the fanatic ones' (p. 245). He relates that kind of psychopathy to the three clusters of personality disorders: one of them is the so-called paranoid group, which consists of schizotypal and paranoid personality disorders. 'The second, comprehending borderline personality, multiple personality and histrionic ones, is contrasted to a third, altogether avoidant: phobic personality disorder and the like' (p. 246).

Throughout recent years some clinical-psychological measures that help to assess different kinds of humour in their relation to normal and pathological conditions were developed. R. Silver (2002, 2007, 2010) introduced a special scale to assess seven different kinds of humour expressed in drawings and narratives:

- lethal and morbid humour, which is diagnosed when respondents express amusement at subjects dying painfully, or being in mortal danger and overtly expressing pain and/or fear, either through words or images;
- lethal, but not morbid humour expressed through amusement at subjects disappearing, dying, or being in mortal danger but not expressing pain and/or fear;
- disparaging humour, when respondents are amused by other subjects who are unlike them and seen as unattractive, frustrated, foolish, or unfortunate, but not in mortal danger;
- self-disparaging humour, when respondents are amused by themselves and perceive themselves as unattractive, frustrated, foolish, or unfortunate, but not in mortal danger;
- ambiguous or ambivalent humour (neutral), when respondents are amused with ambivalent situations, when its outcome is perceived as both negative and positive, or neither negative nor positive, or being unclear;

- resilient humour, when respondents are optimistic and associate themselves with those who are in a positive mood, amused and able to overcome adversity, or when the outcome is hopeful or perceived to be favourable for them;
- playful humour, when respondents are in entirely positive moods and invite others to share their amusement, absurdity, double meaning, or word play; there is no hostility, denial, or covert meanings present in relationships depicted in drawings and narratives.

Silver's presumption was that lethal and morbid humour is more typical for mental pathology, while resilient and playful humour is more linked to mental health. However findings from her own studies (Silver 2002) and from others (Kopytin & Lebedev 2013) indicate that obviously 'normal' and 'pathological' humour hardly exists. Any population is characterised by the mixture of different kinds of humour that can be indicative of different types of personalities with their specific needs and coping strategies as well as social-cultural contexts. The general level of humorous responses is also significant and can serve as one of the characteristics of a population assessed.

According to Silver (2002), different kinds of humour were revealed with the use of her scale in the stimulus drawings of 9 per cent of children aged 9–12 years, 19 per cent of adolescents (aged 13–19 years), 21 per cent of adults aged 20–65 years and 19 per cent of older adults (after 65 years). The average level of humorous responses to one of the drawing tasks, Drawing from Imagination, included in her Silver Drawing Test (SDT), among subjects of different age was 18 per cent. At the same time, males produced significantly more humorous responses than females (24 per cent and 13 per cent, accordingly) and this gender difference was highly significant (chi square = 37.3; $p < 0.01$). In addition, males tended to produce more negative humour than females.

Body and humour in visual arts

While very often humour is represented in the linear form of narration or joke telling, it can be expressed in non-linear, non-verbal forms too. Verbal and visual expression can also be combined to reveal a humorous attitude even more fully, as is typical for comics, cartoons and comedy. As far as certain action or public performance is concerned external appearance and body expression become especially significant, in order to evoke humorous reactions, as is typical in clowning, carnivals, or stage arts.

Both visual and non-visual expressions of humour are abundant in certain ritual practices, religious and seasonal celebrations, such as Halloween, Purim and some others. Real human bodies or imitations of the human form are often given a special place at such events. Various comic figurative representations of the body or its parts made of different materials together with certain actions help people to deal creatively with the dramatic challenges in their collective story, 'dark side' of their body and psyche, to playfully express and transgress their fear of death and rejoice life.

Ambiguous, fantastic, extravagant and often humorous visual representations of the human body, usually combined with different plant and animal forms, are typical for grotesque. Though the original meaning of grotesque was restricted to Ancient Roman decorative style, which was rediscovered and copied by Renaissance artists at the and of the fifteenth century, it has come later to be used as a general adjective for the strange, weird, distorted forms integrating the human body.

A. Remi (2010) believes that beyond the traditional meanings of grotesque as an aesthetic form, it serves as a universal anthropological device, which helps to represent fundamental existential experience of transformation, coming to life and unity.

Though such forms are abundant in many cultures and in different historical periods it appears that comic and grotesque representations of the human body are given a central position in the New Era. Most schools of modernist art, such as expressionism, Dadaism or cubism are characterised by especially strong connections with humorous, fantastic and weird representations of the human body. Post-modernism, with its tendency to deconstruction, goes even further and together with visual representations of the body gives special significance to actions through and with the body. Very often such representations and actions become a means of self-empowerment and of provoking strong reactions in society, especially when controversial social and cultural issues are confronted. The self portraits by Cindy Sherman, and photographs and paintings by Gilbert and George are just a few examples of this.

Humour often plays an important role in artistic endeavors of those who take an active stance in the world and confront the dominant ideology or cultural norms. This was typical, in particular, of a certain segment of Russian non-conformist artists, who openly expressed their disagreement with social realism as a dominant artistic method or communist ideology from 1960s until the collapse of communism.

Very often, creations of outsider artists illustrate various kinds of humour and its ability to help people with certain mental and social difficulties to reveal their creativity, achieve inner integration, cope with paradoxes of their existence and establish their identity.

Body and humour in art therapy

Art therapy was a term first used in the UK and the US in the 1940s, during the post-second world war rehabilitation movement. Two strands developed: one as a sensitive form of art teaching applied in clinical settings and another as an aspect of psychotherapy through art. Today, art therapists are considered to be qualified specialists who have a considerable understanding of visual art processes and an ability to communicate with a wide range of clients both individually and in groups using not only words, but visual, plastic forms as well. Their nonverbal communication with clients was believed to be crucial in developing the therapeutic relationship.

Art therapists provide a secure environment and art materials for their clients and stimulate them to express their ideas and feelings through art. Art therapists also encourage their clients to respond to the art they produce, so that long buried feelings can be understood and acknowledged. Art therapy is often considered to be a dialogue between a client and a therapist mediated by art materials and products. Approaches to art therapy vary depending on the theoretical orientation of therapists who are carefully chosen taking into account organisational considerations as well as clinical, cultural and social-demographic factors.

Examples of humour and its relation to the body in art therapy presented below were selected from our own work with mostly non-psychotic clients: those with neurotic, somatoform and stress-related mental disorders (including post-traumatic stress disorder), mild affective disorders (such as anxiety and depressive states), certain personality disorders, and addictions. Clients participated in group interactive art therapy lasting 1–3 months.

A pro-active approach was taken, with focused activities introduced by the therapist at the beginning of the course, but with an increasing initiative on the part of the group during later sessions. Usually sessions lasted 2½ hours. Each session was structured with warm-up activities, a main art-based activity with discussion, and closure. Basic art materials were available, such as crayons and pastels, coloured pencils, gouache and acrylic paints, and white paper of different sizes.

Group art therapy involved various art-based activities that corresponded with appropriate stages of treatment and group dynamics were aimed at different therapeutic targets. For example, participants created individual and cooperative squiggle drawings that encouraged warming-up, creative stimulation, and the safe release of emotions, and also introduced themselves to the group and presented their current emotional state through drawing on the beginning stage of group art therapy.

When a high enough level of trust and safety as well as the initial psychological disclosure was achieved, various drawing tasks and themes were introduced that helped clients to further disclose and work through their personal issues, express and understand their own self-perception, to express their attitude to others in the group, to talk about their disease and discuss resources, to gain perspective on their past and present life situations and to develop interpersonal skills. Those directives included 'realistic and metaphoric self-portraits,' 'my life line,' 'positive and negative feelings,' 'my resources in the past and present,' 'challenging life situations and how I overcome them,' 'personal coat of arms,' 'my life achievements and goals,' and 'presents I give myself and others'. Issues that arose from group dynamics also were worked through using art-based activities and discussions.

Throughout clients' involvement in the above-mentioned themes and self-directed artistic activity, different kinds of humour, in particular, in relation to the body, were revealed and expressed both in the artworks created as well as in clients' narratives. We noticed certain correlations of humour with the following situations as they gradually unfolded throughout the course of group art therapy:

- humour as an expression of resistance to therapy,
- humour as a means to reduce anxiety and ventilate sexual and aggressive drives,

- humour as a means to reduce frustration related to one's attempt to present symptoms and personal issues,
- humour as a means to establish and defend one's identity,
- humour as a means of self-acceptance and integrating incongruous perceptions of oneself,
- humour as a safe way to release and integrate traumatic memories,
- humour as a means to deal creatively with current social and psychological issues and deconstruct the view of reality imposed by society.

Humour as an expression of resistance to therapy

One group of clients, in which humour was abundant and played a significant role in different stages of therapy, was the group that consisted of war veterans with prevailing stress-related symptoms and complex difficulties of adaptation due to their involvement in military campaigns. This group was initially highly resistant to therapy due to a strongly masculine culture and specific clinical traits, which included high anxiety, irritation, difficulties in relationships, low impulse control, absence of interest in life, tiredness, apathy, feelings of pain and discomfort in the body etc.

The beginning of therapy provoked very high tension in the group, which was often disguised by commentaries full of criticism and self-irony. It was very difficult for clients to start drawing, since it was considered 'childish', or 'not a man's business'. In this situation the therapist often introduced one of the stimulus drawing techniques, when clients were asked to select two pictures and then draw their own picture as a response to those stimuli ('drawing from imagination' task, the 'Silver drawing test') (Silver 2002, 2007).

One client drew a picture he called 'Extraordinary situation' and accompanied it with the following story: 'The hurricane destroyed the city and killed many people. Looters began to rob houses. The Ministry of Extraordinary Situations sent a rescue team and everything was cooled down'.

The picture reflects very high inner tension in the client and his attempt to alleviate it by producing humorous imagery representing a catastrophic event and the following salvation. The picture served as a complex metaphor of his ambivalent attitude towards group art therapy. His drawing style was simple, but expressive enough. The picture was characterised by ambiguous humour. The client seemed to be amused with both negative and positives sides in the situation. There are three human figures in the drawing. It's possible that he identified with the two male figures in the drawing, the robber and the arriving member of a rescue team. The client relaxed as a result of this drawing activity and brief discussion of the subject depicted and made his decision to continue working in the group.

Humour as a means to reduce anxiety and ventilate sexual and aggressive drives

In the same group consisting of war veterans, individual and cooperative squiggle drawing activity was introduced to encourage warming-up, creative stimulation, and the safe release of emotions. During the second session the participants were asked to find a partner, take crayons and paper and start drawing squiggles one after another and then to elaborate on the lines of each other and create one or a series of images.

Though the group participants were initially very sceptical about the directive they got involved in the collaborative drawing. After a couple of minutes the first smiles were noticed. Soon some started to laugh loudly and induced others. Due to their involvement in such collaborative drawing activity participants easily got in touch with each other and appeared to be much more relaxed than in the beginning of the session. Most of them enjoyed the directive and realised that imagery can appear naturally without any conscious efforts or advanced drawing skills. Most pictures made in this session included playful and humorous sexual and aggressive symbols, through which inner tension of the group was released.

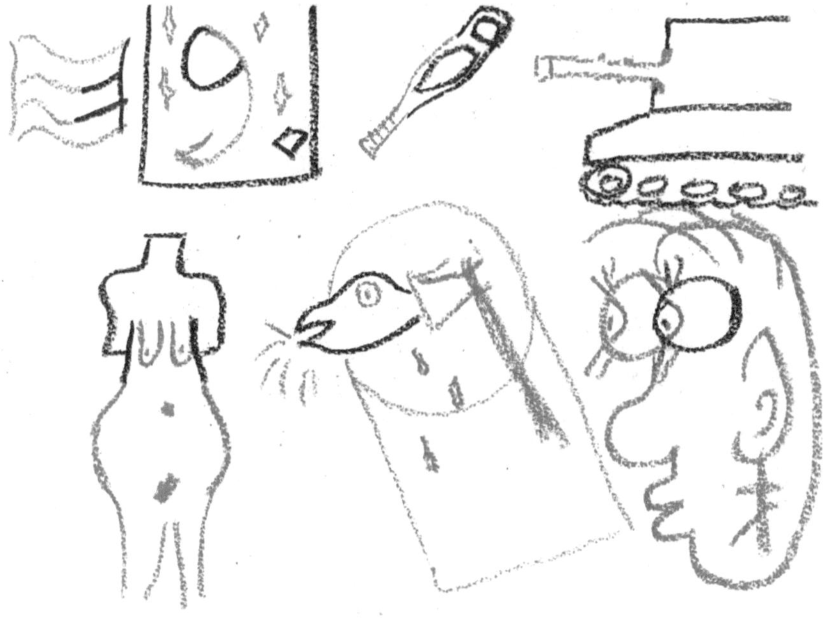

FIGURE 15.1 One of the pictures created as a result of collaborative squiggle drawing

Humour as a means to reduce frustration related to one's attempt to present symptoms and personal issues

In the first several sessions, participants usually begin to carefully present their personal issues and share their symptoms in the group. Most experience obvious difficulties and their anxiety considerably increases, when they confront their 'dark sides'. As far as war veterans are concerned they 'don't want to complain' and are afraid to be perceived as 'a weak person' and not 'a real man'. As one participant wrote in his feedback form at the end of therapy, 'From the first sessions I was afraid … I thought that my personal problems and secrets will be seen to others. I was like a string, which was ready to break…'

Participants are usually invited to draw and present in the group, how they perceive their problems and symptoms. The interesting effect of their attempt to do that using visual means of expression is that they are often able to dissociate from issues presented especially if humour is involved. They overcome their anxious/defensive position and start to relax.

One of the war veterans with somatoform symptoms represented himself and his headache in the form of a hammer beating him on the head. Another one made a grotesque self-portrait expressing himself losing control. Both clients used grotesque and exaggerated body features in attempting to express their perception of psychosomatic or affective disorders and obviously created a comic effect. Such exaggeration helped them to dissociate from the problems presented and keep a more distanced and secure position in this session.

Humour as a means of integrating incongruous perceptions of oneself, and establishing and defending one's identity

Usually when an appropriate level of trust and safety in the group is achieved, participants in more 'mature' groups get ready to disclose and understand their perception of themselves as personalities with a complex of different and often controversial characteristics. Certain prompts, especially such as 'realistic and metaphoric self-portraits,' 'me as a community,' 'my life line,' 'positive and negative feelings,' 'my resources in the past and present', 'personal coat of arms,' and some others help them to carry out this task.

We noticed that humour makes the process of externalising and recognising incongruous perceptions of oneself more efficient and leads to the establishment of a more cohesive self-image, which includes both strengths and weaknesses, but with a prevailing positive self-attitude. It appears that humour also enables cognitive digestion of information related to self-perception and the discovery of some 'core' meanings and values, on which the client's identity is based.

It's not an easy objective, of course, and an appropriate period of time is needed to properly accomplish it. It also requires an appropriate group atmosphere and successful completion of tasks typical for the previous stages of therapy. A certain level of personal maturity in order to be able to cope with the workload of this crucial stage of therapy is needed as well.

A young woman, 23 years old, with organic dissociative disorder (according to ICD-10, the World Health Organization's system, the International Classification of Diseases) participated in the group interactive art therapy at the day psychiatric center. Following the 'me as a community' prompt, she made a picture of herself, which included her four different aspects, or roles, those of a clown, a patient, a little artist, and 'a domestic plant' demonstrating a self-ironic perception of herself. Three of these had a childish appearance, while the fourth one (a patient) looked different. However, the client used certain stereotypical elements, in particular, the mask covering the eyes of the four figures as a protective symbol and a marker of the whole series of pictures.

Different kinds of humour, especially of a self-disparaging and ambiguous nature, were very often expressed in the interactive art therapy group of drug abusers, when they created realistic or metaphorical self-portraits at a crucial stage of therapy. Their natural-size self-portraits were very illustrative in this regard. For instance, a 29-year-old client, who had been using street drugs for about 12 years, represented himself as having strange appearance, with fire in his belly and holding flowers. Though his self-portrait evoked ambiguous feelings while he was presenting it in the group, the client approached it and imitated the posture of the figure on the portrait. This served as an act of self-acceptance and integration of those incongruent qualities that the client dissociated from himself during the previous stage of the session.

During another session in the same group of drug abusers they were asked to select one of the elements of photographic images representing different details of the body, mostly eyes, mouths, hair and hands. Using that detail as a starting point they were invited to elaborate on it following their imagination and create a whole human figure. One of the participants, a 32-year-old woman, made a very expressive picture of a witch sitting on a broom and holding a glass of wine. Though she had no conscious intention to represent herself in the picture and the figure of the woman had no literal resemblance to her, after presenting her picture to the group she agreed that she actually met her inner self due to this activity. It was noticed that mostly the eyes of the woman in her picture looked like her eyes.

Humour as a safe way to release traumatic memories

Humour often appears when clients are getting close to inner splits and traumatic memories and start externalising using artistic means in 'mature' groups. Due to the high level of group cohesion, the therapeutic potential of the group is usually very high as participants stimulate and support each other in their attempts to meet and work through their traumatic past experiences.

In this context, various collaborative whole-group artistic activities can be very helpful. Group painting, in particular, is very potent with this regard and often able to evoke humour in the group, especially, when the group feels enough safety and freedom to materialise its creative ideas. Sometimes those ideas appear to be disturbing, strange, unpleasant or repelling, but nevertheless bring satisfaction, enjoyment and understanding. Humour is often very vividly expressed and again reveals its group-building power as it involves its members in the joint creative activity.

The group consisting of the drug abusers was invited to create a group painting on any theme. The theme of 'garbage pit' was selected as most interesting for the group. It was decided to use any art materials and objects including those brought from the outside to make 'the pit' in the form of a total installation. Participants got very involved in doing that. The floor was covered with paper and many images and texts soon appeared chaotically spread on the paper. After that the group enthusiastically started to search for objects and material outside of the room and arrange them into a huge composition. Some found objects were brought from the territory of the rehabilitation center or from the kitchen and included in the composition, sometimes by the way representing very dramatic past situations. Some of the details included a blood soaked hand cut by an axe, a corpse wrapped in cellophane and thrown onto the garbage pit, a tray with snacks nearby, and a broken refrigerator.

Humour as a means to creatively deal with current social and psychological issues and deconstruct perceptions of reality imposed by society

This is one of the characteristics of the main and final stages of therapy, when critical consideration of clients' past and present social roles and positions and their plans for the future become important subjects. Current social discourses including those related to mass media, political practice and popular culture and their impact on individual self-image are often explored and discussed in the group. In art therapy, all those discourses can be made easily observable and creatively dealt with, if they are presented in a material, visual form, such as magazines, newspapers, posters etc. with their abundant images and texts.

Some artistic activities, which can be implemented in the group, include creating photo collages, making personal or group advertisements and posters and so on. Participants are invited to use different printed media and 'play' with them, in order to deconstruct and construct their different perceptions of reality and possibly find their own, more authentic way of looking and making.

Making collages and working with photographs and texts taken from the printed material can be very illustrative in this regard. One group participant, a 34-year-old woman, made a poster related to the current social-political situation as her response to those questions, which she was trying to resolve while planning her future. She seemed to identify with the man on her poster, who was thinking about some activities, such as creating music, playing in a group, or becoming a star. Suddenly a red apple was falling on his head and a new, revolutionary idea came into his mind. The slogan on the poster said: 'What you can do some day'. The poster seemed to represent her ambivalent attitude to the current social-political situation. However, humour plays a significant role and provides a liberating effect.

Another member of the same group made a poster, which reflected her critical attitude towards consumerist values and false promises offered by mass culture, which makes the human body 'a hostage.' She included a slogan, 'Come to Korobitsino! (a town in the St. Petersburg region), imitating a poster for a ski resort. There are no mountains there in reality, but she drew snow-capped mountains to create an illusion of a fashionable resort. She also drew tubes of toothpaste with another slogan, 'Snow-white of your dream'. People who used this toothpaste and came to Korobitsino were smiling showing their snow-white teeth. Sun-glasses that people on her poster wore had an ambiguous meaning. They made them more comfortable and look more fashionable, resembling 'real' vacationers at popular resorts. At the same time, sun-glasses made them blindfolded.

Conclusion

The role of humour in human culture, everyday life and therapy is very important and sometimes crucial. Humour has multiple relations to the body. It must be embodied to evoke a wide range of humorous responses, to be experienced and rendered. This is true not only with regard to the real, physical body, but also in relation to its different visual representations. This is why art can become a relevant platform to evoke and express humour.

There are many definitions of humour and its different types. Some of them appear to be more related to mental health and resilience, while others seem to be linked to mental pathology. Combining developmental, clinical-psychiatric and social-cultural considerations is necessary for a more balanced understanding of the many positive functions of humour and its therapeutic potential. They include, in particular, such functions as expressing aggression and sexuality, coping with difficult inner and outer situations, intellectual processing of information, inclusion in the social context, revealing one's creative potential, resisting authority, and supporting identity construction.

Art provides an additional, and often more secure and effective, outlet for expressing humour in its relation to the body. Not accidentally, the 'humorous body' is given a very important and often central position in the history of art as well as in contemporary artistic endeavors. Art therapy provides a wide spectrum of possibilities to utilise humour in order to reach an array of therapeutic objectives.

References

Astruc, R. (2010) *Le Renouveau du Grotesque dans le Roman du XX e Siecle: Essai d'Antropologie Litteraire*, Paris: Classiques Garnier.

Bengesser, G. (1998) 'The lacking sense of humor in some psychopaths,' in G. Roux and M. Laharie (eds) *L'Humor: Histoire, Culture et Psychologie*, Paris: SIPE, pp. 245–247.

Damascio, A. (1999) *The Feeling of What Happens: Body and Emotion in the Making of Consciousness*, London: Harcourt Brace and Company.

Dissanayake, E. (1988) *What is Art For?* Seattle and London: University of Washington Press.

Feldenkrais, M. (1950) *Body and Mature Behavior: A Study of Anxiety, Sex, Gravitation and Learning*, New York: International University Press.
Freud, S. (1961a) 'Instincts and their vicissitudes,' in J. Strachey (ed.) *The Standard Edition of the Complete Psychological Works of Sigmund Freud*, vol. 14, London: Hogarth Press, pp. 117–140.
Freud, S. (1961b) 'The ego and the id,' in J. Strachey (ed.) *The Standard Edition of the Complete Psychological Works of Sigmund Freud*, London: Hogarth Press, vol. 19: 3–66.
Ijuin, S. (1998). 'Apathy syndrome and its humor,' in G. Roux and M. Laharie (eds), *L'humour: Histoire, Culture et Psychologie*, Paris: Société Internationale de Psychothérapie de l'Expression et d'Art-Thérapie, pp. 252–254).
Jakab, I. (1998a) 'Humor and psychoanalysis,' in G. Roux and M. Laharie (eds) *L'Humor: Histoire, Culture et Psychologie*, Paris: SIPE, pp. 15–22.
Jakab, I. (1998b) 'Children's humor', in G. Roux and M. Laharie (eds) *L'Humor: Histoire, Culture et Psychologie*, Paris: SIPE, pp. 77–82.
Kopytin, A. and Lebedev, A. (2013) 'Humor, self-attitude, emotions and cognitions in group art therapy with war veterans', *Art Therapy: Journal of the American Art Therapy Association*, 30(1): 20–29.
McDougal, J. (1989) *Theatres of the Body*, London: Free Association Books.
Nagy, J. (1998) 'Anxiety, depression and humor,' in G. Roux and M. Laharie (eds) *L'Humor: Histoire, Culture et Psychologie*, Paris: SIPE, pp. 255–257.
Reich, W. (1972) *Character Analysis*, New York: Touchstone.
Roux, G. and Laharie, M. (eds.) (1998) *L'Humor: Histoire, Culture et Psychologie*, Paris: SIPE.
Seiichi, I. (1998) 'Apathy syndrome and its humor', in G. Roux and M. Laharie (eds.) *L'Humor: Histoire, Culture et Psychologie*, Paris: SIPE, pp. 252–255.
Silver, R. (2002) *Three Art Assessments*, New York: Brunner-Routledge.
Silver, R. (2007) *The Silver Drawing Test and Draw-a-Story*, New York: Routledge.
Silver, R. (2010) *Identifying Risks for Aggression and Depression Through Metaphors: The Mouse, The Bride and the Use of Humor*, Dewitt, NY: Purple Finch Press.
Verdeau-Pailles, J. (1998) 'L'humour en psychiatrie et en psychopathologie', in G. Roux and M. Laharie (eds.) *L'Humor: Histoire, Culture et Psychologie*, Paris: SIPE, pp. 23–41.
Ziv, A. (1984) *Personality and Sense of Humor*, New York: Springer.

INDEX